Arts and Entrepreneurship

Arts and Entrepreneurship

Edited by
J. Mark Munoz and Julienne W. Shields

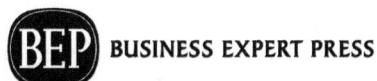

Arts and Entrepreneurship

First published in 2018 by
Business Expert Press, LLC
222 East 46th Street, New York, NY 10017
www.businessexpertpress.com

ISBN-13: 978-1-63157-633-1 (paperback)
ISBN-13: 978-1-63157-634-8 (e-book)

Business Expert Press Entrepreneurship and Small Business Management Collection

Collection ISSN: 1946-5653 (print)
Collection ISSN: 1946-5661 (electronic)

Cover and interior design by Exeter Premedia Services Private Ltd., Chennai, India

First edition: 2018

10 9 8 7 6 5 4 3 2 1

Printed in the United States of America.

Abstract

Interest in entrepreneurship in the arts has grown in recent years. Artists need to look past their product and service, and leverage resources under risk and uncertainty to seize opportunities and optimize gains. Strategic entrepreneurial and management approaches when converged with a passion for the arts, can lead business enterprises into new and exciting frontiers. This book brought together experts and thought leaders from around the world to uncover business success strategies for art enthusiasts worldwide.

Keywords

arts, arts and entrepreneurship, entrepreneurship

Contents

Introduction

J. Mark Munoz and Julienne W. Shields

Introduction

Over the past centuries, people all over the world have used their talents and abilities to make art. Some utilized their artistic tendencies to follow a passion to create. Others leveraged their creative abilities to generate income for themselves and their families. Whatever the reason, thousands of different forms of art are created every day.

Evidence of art is everywhere—museums, arts, and crafts being sold in the streets by vendors, clothing designs, graffiti on the walls, advertising signs and billboards, music, theater and movie productions, and many more.

Art unleashes the creative spirit of people and is expressed in diverse forms. In profound ways, it adds to the beauty and glamour of the world in which we live.

For people who want to build on a career, lifestyle, or body of work within artistic industries, countless challenges emerge. The hard questions include: how can I generate a sustainable income stream from my creative work? Do I give emphasis on my artistic purpose or the marketability of my work? How can I effectively manage a business enterprise—personally or with agents or partners? How do I balance the demands of my artistry along with the demands of the business?

Artist entrepreneurs tend to differentiate their discipline from artisan endeavors and crafts—which are more commercial. Emphasis for artisans is frequently placed on design, efficiency, or efficacy focusing on the customer's wants and needs rather than the artist's creative pursuits, vision and voice.

It is often difficult to find a balance between one's artistic integrity and the need be financially secure. It is not uncommon to hear the term "starving artist" to depict a person who pursues a passion for his or her craft without finding commercial success.

Fortunately, the term "starving artist" is being increasingly rejected through action as new enterprising frameworks develop the entrepreneurial mindset of emerging artists.

This book aims to encourage artists all over the world to understand the notion of arts entrepreneurship and hone their entrepreneurial abilities. With an assembled team of experts from disparate countries, this book provides ideas and fresh insights on how to converge artistic and entrepreneurial intent.

Understanding Arts Entrepreneurship

Originating from the French word "*entreprendre*" meaning "*to undertake,*" entrepreneurship has become a by-word to describe the process of operating an enterprise despite constraints relating to risk and uncertainty. It has been described in the context of "*pursuit of opportunity beyond resources controlled*" (Stevenson, Roberts, and Grousbeck 1989), driver of innovation and economic advancement (Schumpeter 1934), and associated with risk-propensity (Brockhaus 1980). Perhaps Babson College's definition "a way of thinking and acting that is opportunity obsessed, holistic in approach, and leadership balanced," is particularly viable for the artist entrepreneur. There is no exact formula for entrepreneurship, since it is anchored on uniqueness and individuality (Hoque 2014).

Entrepreneurship plays a key role in the arts (Henry 2007). Business acumen sets the foundation for financially successful art enterprises, but it is also grounded in quality, desirability, and the artist's ability to connect with intent with meaning for the viewer, audience, listener, participant, and so on. Artists who have the ability to brand and market themselves well eventually develop a large and steady set of clients that make their ventures sustainable.

Artist entrepreneurs can be found in many *business* fields and disciplines. There is a diversity of options available for the artistically inclined. For instance, arts organizations can be found in the performing arts and museums and cultural industries such as those in film, music, and video games (Colbert 2007).

Arts enterprises have been in existence for centuries. Art can be traced to prehistoric times and have been evident in cave paintings. Craft firms have been noted as early as the Medieval period (Heslop 1997).

There are several attributes that characterizes art enterprises:

Anchored on individual artistry—ventures anchored on the arts, typically has one or more individuals who leverage their artistic talents and abilities. Personalization is a defining attribute of artistic firms (Svejenova, Planellas, and Vives 2010).

Grounded on integrity—arts enterprises often require high level of trust and sincerity. Reputation and trust are important considerations in artistic firms (Moulin 1967). For artists, maintaining their artistic integrity is an important part of their craft.

Diversity in forms, approaches and sizes—given the multitude of ways in which art can be created and sold, the practice of art entrepreneurship come in many shapes, forms and sizes. Jeffcutt, Pick, and Protherough (2000) observed that sizes of creative industries range from micro-level to ones that are trans-national.

Operationally complex—arts enterprises often need to deal with conflicting forces. For instance, should emphasis be placed on artistic integrity or commercial viability? On top of these challenges, a keen understanding of markets is not easy. This complexity transcends into the way artisan ventures and artistic ventures operate. Artisan ventures simply create products for customers, while artistic ventures offer a higher level of control over the outcome. Caves (2006) indicated that industries with creative flair tend to be characterized by: (1) uncertain demand, (2) require skilled inputs, (3) infinite variety, (4) vertically differentiated, and (5) durability.

Follows a growth and development trajectory—the skills of artists shift over time. Artists typically go through a period of apprenticeship to gain expertise in their craft (Caves 2006). In most cases, artists simply become better over time. Arts enterprises need to manage these changes and growth. The environment in which the artist lives in (i.e., economic, political, and social) influences their art and changes them while allowing them to also influence the world they live in.

Evolving by nature—as artistic preferences can evolve over time, arts ventures tend to be in flux and continue to change. Art created at a particular moment in time is not only a reflection of the artist but also a characterization of the era in which it takes place. Creative industries have evolved over the past 30 years (Healy 2002).

Global appeal—interest in arts enterprises transcend borders. The advent of technological advances and globalization has rapidly internationalized art. E-commerce has set the foundation for artists to sell their craft across multiple channels and internationally (Zwahlen 2010).

Challenges

Operating arts enterprises can be challenging. Typical barriers include: defining "arts entrepreneurship" compared to creative industries, artisanship, and so on. Artists need to also consider from where the inspiration flows. There is a need to compartmentalize commercial activities and artistic activities to achieve a degree of authenticity. Other challenges include:

Overlapping roles—Emerging artist entrepreneurs need to multitask specially in the start-up stages (Sachar 2011). Several tasks need to be completed and many entrepreneurs lose track of priorities.

Financial pressures—Like many microenterprises, arts enterprises need to generate income early in their development stage. Microenterprises in the craft industry need to carefully plan their marketing strategy (Kean, Niemeyer, and Miller 1996). The ability to attract customers and convert these customers into paying patrons is critical.

Changing consumer taste—Consumer preferences change over time. Keeping abreast with changes is important. Arts enterprises need to be cognizant of environmental changes taking place such as those that impact their audience, costs and revenues among others (Culbert et al. 1996).

Balancing creativity and profitability—Arts enterprises need to find the right spot that suits their creative drive while staying profitable. High emphasis on management can dampen an artists' creativity (Hodsoll 1985).

Declining support—There is a lot of competition for donors and sponsors, clientele, audiences, grant opportunities, and so on. Economic challenges can also dampen enthusiasm in the arts and the philanthropic spirit. Cultural organizations have faced public funding cuts and intense sponsorship competition (Colbert 2007).

Research and resource limitations—Limited ability to gather the right information at the right time can pose difficulties. For instance, in arts enterprise internationalization, challenges include resource limitations, lack of information and access to business advise (Leeke 1994).

Finding suitable mentors—Mentors are essential in the craft industry (Becker 2006) and for artist entrepreneurs—many of whom do not have formal business training or networks on which to rely. Finding the right business coach and mentor is not always easy.

Opportunities

Arts enterprises offer a lot of potential for business success. These enterprises also can have an impact on local economies. Their roles and impact include:

Job creators—Thousands of jobs are created by arts enterprises. Creative industries are employment generators (Foord 2008).
Sustainable self-employment is what many artists strive for. It allows for creative freedom in authentic ways over time. And artistic trends are to collaborate which generates work among networks of artists.

Economic growth—Arts enterprises stimulate economic activities. Creative industries are important economic foundations (Hartley 2005).

Stimulate innovation—the creative nature of arts enterprises sets the stage for innovative thinking. Creative industries sets the stage for innovation and development in regions (Bilton 2007).

Attract donors and investors—Art patrons abound worldwide. Arts enterprises have traditionally received significant support from philanthropists. There are diverse sources for funding for performing arts ranging from philanthropy (36 percent), government (6 percent), others (58 percent) (Mulcahy 1999).

Opportunity for internationalization—The global nature of arts enterprises opens doors for the pursuit of international initiatives and partnerships. There has been rising interest in selling crafts internationally (Knott 1994; Fillis 2000).

Given the growing importance of the topic and the opportunities it presents, the editors decided to pursue this book project and bring together thought leaders, experts and practitioners to share their views on arts and entrepreneurship.

Book Objectives and Organization

The editors hope this book project will serve as a guide book that will help artists from around the world navigate the complex world of business and uncover pathways to success. The book covers diverse topics that are intended to educate the reader in different aspects of arts entrepreneurship.

The intent of the book is to provide a blend of theoretical and practical knowledge on the subject. The editors hope that the book will be valuable to a broad range of art enthusiasts including students, academics, artists, entrepreneurs, executives, consultants, government leaders, and policy makers.

The book also takes on a highly international perspective. The editors believe that the practice of arts entrepreneurship takes place all over the world. Viewpoints of experts from several international locations are woven into the book.

The book is organized in five sections. **Section 1** is **Introduction** (*J. Mark Munoz and Julienne W. Shields*). **Section 2** pertains to **Understanding Arts Entrepreneurship** and includes the following chapters The value(s) of arts business (*Per Darmer, Joobin Ordoobody and Alireza Saify*), We are not a commercial firm (*Deirdre McQuillan*), and Creating value in the performing arts industries: A process for arts entrepreneurs (*Sara Theis and Mark C. Samples*). **Section 3** is **Arts Culture, Values and Internationalization** with chapters including Cultural embeddedness in the arts (*Deirdre Mcquillan*), Art entrepreneurship and internationalization at home: Internationalization strategies of theaters from a Central European country (*Pareskevi Karageorgu and Andreja Jaklic*). **Section 4** pertains to **Pathways to Growth and Success** and includes Exploring the emergence of contemporary art galleries in Istanbul: The effectuation perspective (*Aytug Sozuer*), ARTrepreneurship: Shifting to a business mindset in a creative world (*Sonia BasSheva Mañjon and Melissa Crum*), Development of performance-based class projects in the arts

(*Larry Stapleton and J. Mark Munoz*), The entrepreneurial development of self-employed artists (*Robert Moussetis*), and Strategic thinking in arts entrepreneurship (*Todd Stuart*). **Section 5** is the **Conclusion** (*J. Mark Munoz and Julienne W. Shields*).

With a growingly complex global business world, with rigorous demands on time and talent, the editors hope that this book provides the foundation for the future success of artist entrepreneurs. There is much room to further theoretical and practical knowledge on the topic of arts entrepreneurship. Success in arts entrepreneurship can enrich lives, stimulate economies, and add truth, beauty and glamor to the world.

References

Becker, H.S. 2006. "The Work Itself." In *Art from Start to Finish: Jazz, Painting, Writing, and Other Improvisations*, eds. H.S. Becker, R.R. Faulkner, and B. Kirshenblatt-Gimblett, 21–30. Chicago, IL: University of Chicago.

Bilton, C. 2007. *Management and Creativity*. Oxford: Blackwell.

Brockhaus, R. 1980. "Risk-Taking Propensity of Entrepreneurs." *Academy of Management Journal* 23, no. 3, pp. 509–20.

Caves, R.E. 2006. "Economic Analysis and Steps Toward Completing the Work." In *Art from Start to Finish: Jazz, Painting, Writing, and Other Improvisations*, eds. H.S. Becker, R.R. Faulkner, and B. Kirshenblatt-Gimblett, 135–48. Chicago, IL: University of Chicago.

Colbert, F. 2007. *Le Marketing des Arts et de la Culture*. Montreal: Gaetan Morin Editeur.

Culbert, J., W.M. Keens, L. Lewis, and T. Wolf. 1996. *Rethinking Stabilization: Strengthening Arts Organizations During Times of Change*. Cambridge, MA: Strategic Grantmaker Services.

Fillis, I. 2000. An Examination of the Internationalization Process of the Smaller Craft Firm in the United Kingdom and the Republic of Ireland. Unpublished PhD thesis. Stirling, Scotland: University of Stirling.

Foord, J. 2008. "Strategies for Creative Industries: An International Review." *Creative Industries Journal* 1, pp. 91–113.

Hartley, J. 2005. "Creative Industries." In *The Creative Industries*, ed. J. Hartley, 1–40. Oxford: Blackwell.

Healy, K. 2002. "What's New for Culture in the New Economy?" *Journal of Arts Management Law and Society* 32, no. 2, pp. 86–103.

Henry, C. (ed.). 2007. *Entrepreneurship in the Creative Industries: An International Perspective*. Cheltenham: Edward Elgar.

Heslop, T.A. 1997. "How Strange the Change from Major to Minor: Hierarchies and Medieval Art." In *The Culture of Craft*, ed. P. Dormer. Manchester: Manchester University Press.

Hodsoll, F. 1985. "The National Endowment for the Arts and Cultural Economics: The Information Partnership." *Journal of Cultural Economics* 9, no. 1, pp. 1–12.

Hoque, F. 2014. Defining the Word "Entrepreneur" for the 21st Century. Available at http://cnn.com/2014/11/20/living/ivory-tower-community-colleges/index.html?iref=allsearch (accessed November 23, 2014).

Jeffcutt, P., J. Pick, and R. Protherough. 2000. "Culture and Industry: Exploring the Debate." *Studies in Cultures, Organizations and Societies* 6, no. 2, pp. 129–43.

Kean, R.C., S. Niemeyer, and N.J. Miller. 1996. "Competitive Strategies in the Craft Product Retailing Industry." *Journal of Small Business Management* 34, no. 1, pp. 13–23.

Knott, C.A. 1994. *Crafts in the 1990s: A Socio-Economic Study of Craftspeople in England, Scotland and Wales*. London: Crafts Council.

Leeke, D. 1994. *Audit of the Craft Sector in Northern Ireland*. Completed for Craftworks NI (Ltd), Belfast.

Moulin, R. 1967. Le march_e de la peinture en France. Paris: Les_Editions Minuit.

Mulcahy, K.V. 1999. "Cultural Patronage in the United States." *International Journal of Arts Management* 2, no. 1, pp. 53–58.

Sachar, C. 2011. "Quit Your Day Job: Creative with Clay. Available at www.etsy.com/blog/en/2011/quit-your-day-job-creative-with-clay/ (accessed August 8, 2012).

Schumpeter, J. 1934. *The Theory of Economic Development*. Cambridge, MA: Harvard University Press.

Stevenson, H., M. Roberts, and H. Grousbeck. 1989. *New Business Ventures and the Entrepreneur*. Homewood, IL: Irwin.

Svejenova, S., M. Planellas, and L. Vives. 2010. "An Individual Business Model in the Making: A Chef's Quest for Creative Freedom." *Long Range Planning* 43, nos. 2–3, pp. 408–30.

Zwahlen, C. 2010. Independent Artisans are Crowding onto the Web. *Los Angeles Times*, March 1.

PART I

Understanding Arts Entrepreneurship

CHAPTER 1

The Value(s) of Arts Business

Joobin Ordoobody, Alireza Saify, and Per Darmer

Art conventionally can be defined as the expression of one's emotions and insights through formalist representations that inspire imagination (Adajian 2007; for a full discussion look at Dickie 1969; Rosenberg 1983; D'Azevedo 1958), where the key is the artist's style, imagination, or inner feelings. Conversely, business is largely associated with commercial activities which concern economic profitability, market share, and wealth accumulation (Porter 2008; also look at Schumpeter 1934), where a lot of weight is put on the consumer (Friedman 2016). Thus, the two seem to have paradoxes in raison d'être that result in conflicting values. For an artist, the unique aesthetic or sociocultural value of his creation might be the prominent aspect of production. Yet, there are industrial aspects to the arts which contribute to the complexity of its production.

For many artists, the continuity of style, philosophy, and values might be prioritized over economic salience of the entrepreneurship. In other words, securing the continuity of their style and values over extended organizational life cycles will be of a greater importance over profitability. However, the industrial side of production is increasingly dominating arts and entertainment through large-scale commercialization and internationalization mechanisms. Famous Chilean filmmaker, Alejandro Jodorowsky, clearly addresses this pressure after failing to find sufficient support from professional investors and turning to people on social media to finance his project:

"…Hollywood films that have colonized the entire world. They have taken over the theaters. They have taken over advertising and distribution.

What is left there for someone like me… who thinks cinema is arts? Nothing." (JodorowskyFilms 2017).

Jodorowsky is not the only filmmaker who is aware of this trend. Cinema indeed seems to be an extreme case where industrial values are broadly salient. David Lynch makes similar comments about his struggle in cinema:

> Things changed a lot… So many films were not doing well at the box office even though they might have been great films and the things that were doing well at the box office weren't the things that I would want to do. (Stolworthy 2017)

Despite institutions that put additional pressures on artistic values of production, however, it is possible to switch between the role of an entrepreneur and an artist, to reconcile the two aspects of production. According to Abbas Kiarostami, a world-class filmmaker whose work has once brought him Palme d'Or, this is another force that has blurred the boundaries between art and business throughout the history of cinema:

> I don't think we sort it out in one definition or in words. I think the real question, which can be frustrating or satisfying is to what extent, cinema, when it was born was meant to be lead where it is now, its present state; that's what I really wonder. We also need to know where is the border between cinema as an art and cinema as a business. (The Modern School of Film 2016)

In this chapter, the authors will present an overview of different approaches that artists may take in face of institutional pressures that promote industrial values and address how some of them redefine entrepreneurship in doing so. To provide descriptions about such mechanisms, archival resources about Iranian filmmakers are used.

Artist (or) Entrepreneur

Although the concept of entrepreneurship has been primarily developed in business studies, it has a fundamental tie to arts at its core. Considering the classical definitions of entrepreneurship, it has been described as "making a major change in methods of manufacturing, producing new products and creating new industries" (Schumpeter 2003, p. 132). The entrepreneurs also have been introduced as those who have tendency to manage and operate a business unit and handle pertaining risks to make profit (Business Dictionary 2017). Besides these sorts of definitions which are rooted in economic and commercial traditions of entrepreneurship, there are others that consider factors such as values or creating an experience rather than cost and benefit. Particularly, when it comes to the arts, entrepreneurship means findings new artistic concepts, adopting methods of storytelling and using organizational structures as means of expressions to publicize the artistic ideas. In this context, managing environmental pressures and limitations (rather than revenue generation and wealth accumulation) are the main purpose of entrepreneurial activities (Scherdin and Zander 2011, p. 3). There is a notable distinction between adventure capitalists and entrepreneurs, where the former is an (often wealthy) individual finding interest in a project or idea, who "meets with persons who wish to oversee and execute the project, and makes a decision on whether or not to extend funding to the endeavor" (Dass 2009). An art entrepreneur is an individual who assumes ownership over a particular entrepreneurial style, idea, and process in the field of arts. Entrepreneurial activities in many of the arts even require "passion"; a passion that transcends financial considerations (Darmer 2008).

The Institutional Context of the Arts

If not more, the relationship between an artistic production and its institutional environment is not any less critical than the elements of ownership, style, and passion. Institutions are defined as "humanly devised codes of behavior" (North 1990) which might introduce or enforce some "recipes" (Walsh 1995) for the standard production into a field. Indeed, art has been an inspiring subject for some of the greatest institutional scholars such as DiMaggio, or even before him, Pierre Bourdieu who introduced the concept of field (Bourdieu 1969) which is an appropriate level of analysis for the study of institutions and organizations (DiMaggio and Powell 1983; Hinings and Greenwood 2002) and has a considerable history in the studies of cultural production—(an organizational field is a set of organizations that "in the aggregate, constitute a recognized area of institutional life" (DiMaggio and Powell 1983, p. 148).

Accordingly art may be defined as "(1) an artifact (2) a set of the aspects of which has had conferred upon it the status of candidate for appreciation by some person or persons acting on behalf of a certain social institution (the art world)." (Dickie 1974; also look at Yanal 1998; Dickie 1969; DiMaggio 1987). The second part of this definition is what can substantially link arts with more recent accounts of entrepreneurship, in which "creating" legitimacy for innovative ideas in a "revitalizing society" stands central to the definition of entrepreneurship (Berglund, Dahlin, and Johansson 2007). Hence, establishing social acceptance or appreciation of (at least) key individuals who represent the support of significant social institutions or streams (i.e., the gatekeepers) is critical. Before discussing the ways of attaining such support, it is worthwhile to further tap into the nuances in the institutional context of artistic production.

Institutional settings and interactions vary across time and space. More precisely, institutions and their interactions among various actors, across markets and field configuring events (such as festivals or reviews in the media) form different production regimes. Each regime signifies a different set of logics, rules, and gatekeepers. Field configuring events are key to the stability or change of balance, policies, and structure of the field (for a full discussion look at Moeran and Pedersen 2011; Mazza and Pedersen 2004). As a result, each regime provides a different reference point for an author to establish the legitimacy of his/her work.

The Case of Iranian Cinema

Cinema is definitely no exception when it comes to variations in production context. In an author cinema where production is regarded as artistic creation/expression to convey "the mark of and refine the author's personal style," critics play the central role in provision of sufficient acceptance among other related institutions. Hence, an author (usually the director) who achieves the approval of critics and colleagues will be often able to obtain the necessary resources for production and remain the central decision maker in the production process. In a studio system, however, the individual or corporate producer oversees overall aspects of a production, oftentimes linking separate scriptwriter and directors to each other. Hence, a scriptwriter or director has the challenge of convincing a producer and his resources would be limited to the degree that the project may achieve box office results and foster profitability. Yet, there is another production regime in cinema, perhaps establishing a middle ground between the first two, usually referred to as national cinema. In this regime, cinema is valued as media, providing mass communication on cultural and national issues. Hence, author, scriptwriter, and producer have to interact, often under the guiding policies of an overseeing institution, to not only meet box office standards to an acceptable extent, but also promote dialogue on cultural, social, or political issues of national significance. Therefore, production would be considered legitimate when it sufficiently draws the attention of the target audience and meets the conditions of overseeing protocols and policies (Mathieu and Strandvad 2009).

While one type of these mechanisms might dominate a specific field or even a whole country's industry (depending on the dominant mode of production in that country), it does not necessitate exclusion of the other types. Iranian cinema is a good example in which the traces of all three streams are present. The structure of the industry is traditionally established around the author system, as is the working style of elder well-known Iranian filmmakers. For example, Masoud Kimiayi clearly elaborates on the central role of an author in response to a journalist who raised the speculation about the editing of his last movie, "The Domestic Murderer":

"Is such a thing possible that it would have a different cut? ... The movie is mine! [Pause.] The movie, its economy is his [points to the producer], its being is mine." (CaffeCinema 2017)

Kimiayi's claim was later backed up in the same conference by a colleague, Fereydoon Jeyrani, who was called and introduced to the audience as "the talking history of Iranian cinema":

I came here to support Mr. Kimiayi [the director], and to express to Mr. Kimiayi that the author of the film is director, and the director of the film is the author of the film. It is the author or director who can decide, everywhere around the world, about what to do.

I do not want to underestimate the role of producer, producer has a fundamental role in formation of the movie... Hence, I came here tonight to definitely tell you that all the friends present in here are backing the director. (CaffeCinema 2017)

Indeed, Jeyrani is not the only person who backs up Kimiayi. Javad Toosi, a well-known Iranian critic and an admirer of Kimiayi's art, has an exclusive look on this author in his writing (Saemi 2017). Kimiayi's strong network of like-minded professionals, fans, and numerous actors and actresses who are fond of his artistic style allows Kimiayi to talk even more strictly to the producer in a press conference:

"The film is short or long, or it is this way or that way, we will cut it shorter, is not your level." (CaffeCinema 2017)

Kimiayi goes even further to indicate that standing beside him is the actual source of legitimacy:

Mr. Ghouchani is respected, his occupation was in advertising, still is, and he knows it very well. With producing this movie, he had a big advertising [campaign] for himself, beside me, taking pictures, news, it just went on until it was near end. (CaffeCinema 2017)

Yet, despite all the credit that Kimiayi holds in Iranian cinema, the producer's hope and attempt to raise a controversy in a press conference at Fajr Festival[1] highlights the significance of field configuring events in the distribution of legitimacy and power within a field.

An old friend and colleague of Kimiayi, Abbas Kiarostami, however, had a quite different approach with the author regime. His movies often casted amateurs and had a small crew. With his well-known minimalist, documentary-like style, along with early adoption of digital cinematography in Iran, he was not in need of large budgets. Hence, he could remain the main process owner in all aspects of production. Moreover,

---

[1] The largest national film festival.

he diversified his market overseas and always tried to take advantage of international festivals:

> Festivals have had a subconscious effect on me; it is a positive thing to be acclaimed and approved which makes you self confident and brave for experiencing new things; something that is rare in Iran and most of the time when a movie varies in accepted norms and scales from other products, it would face the critics' parochialism and lacking of knowledge. These critics are sometimes so influential that could affect public and even movie producers' opinion. Outside of Iran, film reviewers have been more accurate and make the filmmakers more self confident; however, I should mention that I have never attempted to change my methods of filmmaking according to the attitudes of foreigner critics. Actually, due to the fact that the form of my artwork is determined by the subject and its content, I am not able to change my style of work in the way that the western reviewers or festivals prefer... (Hashemi 2016).

As mentioned before, however, author regime is not the only system of filmmaking in Iran. As a recent graduate of Soureh University, Saeed Roostai started his feature-film career with a script for which he kept contacting producers to the point of frustration. When finally a producer offered support, however, his first film acquired almost all of the awards at Fajr Festival and brought him the admiration of many critics as well as a remarkable box office performance (Azarpanah 2016). Yet, in his next attempt, he has worked with a different producer and taken only the role of scriptwriter. Due to his talent in meeting the expectations of audience as well as critics, he is trying to take advantage of working in different roles with different producers in a similar setting to the studio system.

Soureh University also hosts one of the most controversial Iranian critics, Masoud Farasati, as an instructor. Farasati has made strict comments about the works of all the aforementioned filmmakers. He is also the official analyst of the most successful TV show on Iranian cinema, Seven. During the 2016 Fajr Festival, Farasati and Seven, along with a number of other dissatisfied parties took position against the nomination procedures of the festival. The resonance of this conflict in the TV show divided film professionals in opposing groups and raised a lot of controversy. At the closing ceremony, Vahid Jalilvand clearly addressed and condemned the role of national TV during his talk about receiving the best director award:

> National media, Seven, Afkhami, Farasati (the host of the show), you tried all you could to make us [who work in cinema] sulky to each other, but …I hugged [Mohammad Hossein] Mahdavian… You tried to create differences among us, but we like each other, all of us, all of us like each other. Thank you. (CaffeCinema 2017)

Mohammad Hossein Mahdavian was active among the objecting group and with media coverage from Seven and newspapers; he and Jalilvand were emerging as icons of the two opposing groups. Though in their movies, both are using themes that may fit into national cinema, Mahdavian's work which was about political tensions of 80s in Iran, similar to his previous movie which was about Iraq war, was more explicitly supported by official national media such as the Seven show (Seven 2017).

Mahdavian works in teams with writers and producers to raise important sociopolitical conversations, especially in order to convey certain revolutionary values to the younger generation, in coordination with authorities and policy makers (both directly through the connections of producers and indirectly through the support of national media). Therefore, with a desirable performance in the national box office, his work can be considered an effective example of national cinema. This approach enables Mahdavian to stay at the center of attention, be influential on the trends of field configuring events, and accordingly access valuable resources for production. For instance, despite the controversy surrounding his movie in the 2016 Fajr Festival, it was awarded the best film. As the administration of the festival remained under question, the head of Cinema Organization was dismissed, while those involved in the Seven show expressed satisfaction regarding their influence:

> The audience of Seven, with a very large number, defended its approach, that what you did was bringing in a conversation, for the first time, a TV show managed [to do so]. It is five years that

I am [working in] Seven... We were never, in the context of the festival, as successful. That is we have been able to promote both film reviews... as well as discussions among the audience. We should indicate this, if not, then it might seem that our [opposing] friends were so successful in destroying [our] work. Not at all. (Seven 2017)

Conclusion

The complexities of art entrepreneurship were addressed by portraying the conflicting values and conceptual similarities of art and entrepreneurship. Accordingly, institutional accounts of art and entrepreneurship were discussed to connect the two concepts. The role of gatekeepers, field configuring events, and other sources of legitimacy in each production regime was explained. In order to succeed, art entrepreneurs have to find and understand at least one production regime, within which they can plan to attain necessary resources and the support of gatekeeper(s). Festivals might serve as a useful resource in this regard. Moreover, while in institutional scholarship, institutional logics and pressures might be considered omnipresent in a nation's given industry, it was shown how variations of those configurations might coexist within the same space. Future research might address the details of such coexistence.

References

Adajian, T. 2007. *The Definition of Art*. October 23. https://plato.stanford.edu/entries/art-definition/ (accessed June 10, 2017).

Azarpanah, F. 2016. ابد و یک روز را نخوانده رد کردند! March 11. http://hamshahrionline.ir/details/327913/cinema/iraniancinema (accessed June 10, 2017).

Berglund, K., M. Dahlin, and A.W Johansson. 2007. "Walking a Tightrope Between Artistry and Entrepreneurship: The Stories of the Hotel Woodpecker, Otter Inn and Luna Resort." *Journal of Enterprising Communities: People and Places in the Global Economy* 1, no. 3, pp. 268–84.

Bourdieu, P. 1969. "Intellectual Field and Creative Project." *International Social Science Council* 8, no. 2, pp. 89–119.

Business Dictionary. 2017. *Entrepreneur*. http://businessdictionary.com/definition/entrepreneur.html (accessed May 01, 2017).

CaffeCinema. 2017. نشست رسانه ای فیلم "قاتل اهلی" مسعود کیمیایی. February 05. http://aparat.com/v/IVUfw (accessed June 11, 2017).

D'Azevedo, W.L. 1958. "A Structural Approach to Esthetics: Toward a Definition of Art in Anthropology." *American Anthropologist* 60, no. 4, pp. 702–14.

Darmer, P. 2008. "Entrepreneurs in Music: The Passion of Experience Creation." In *Creating Experiences in the Experience Economy*, eds. J. Sundbo and P. Darmer, 111–33. Cheltenham: Edward Elgar Pub.

Dass, C.M. 2009. "Adventure Capitalizing in Baghdad: An Entrepreneurial Approach to Reconstructing Iraq." *Entrepreneurial Business Law Journal* 4, no. 1, pp. 157–84.

Dickie, G. 1969. "Defining Art." *American Philosophical Quarterly* 6, no. 3, pp. 253–356.

Dickie, G. 1974. "What Is Art? An Institutional Analysis." In *Art and the Aesthetic: An Institutional Analysis*, ed. G. Dickie, 171–82. New York: Cornell University Press.

DiMaggio, P. 1987. "Classification in Art." *American Sociological Review* 52, no. 4, pp. 440–55.

DiMaggio, P. and W. W. Powell. 1983. "The Iron Cage Revisited: Institutional Isomorphism and Collective Rationality in Organizational Fields." *American Sociological Review* 48(2), pp. 147–60.

Friedman, M. 2016. *A Theory of the Consumption Function*. Pickle Partners Publishing.

Hashemi, R. 2016. *Abbas Kiarostami Rare Interview Cannes 1997*. July 11. https://youtube.com/watch?v=msZ5Ps-RLPs (accessed June 10, 2017).

Hining, C.R., and R. Greenwood. 2002. "Disconnects and Consequences in Organization Theory." *Administrative Science Quarterly* 47, no. 3, pp. 411–21.

JodorowskyFilms. 2017. *Alejandro Jodorowsky's Call for Action—Endless Poetry (Poesía Sin Fin)*. August 6. https://youtube.com/watch?v=i2d8fdUENMA&t=1s (Accessed June 10, 2017).

Mathieu, C., and S.M. Strandvad. 2009. "Is this What We Should be Comparing When Comparing Film Production Regimes? A Systematic Typological Scheme and Application." *Creative Industries Journal* 1, no. 2, pp. 171–92.

Mazza, C., and J.S. Pedersen. 2004. "From Press to E-Media? The Transformation of an Organizational Field." *Organization Studies* 25, no. 6, pp. 875–96.

Modern School of Film. 2016. *The Modern School of Film with Abbas Kiarostami*. July 17. https://youtube.com/watch?v=cKCabzXgxso (accessed June 15, 2017).

Moeran, B., and J.S. Pedersen. 2011. *Negotiating Values in the Creative Industries: Fairs, Festivals and Competitive Events*. Cambridge: Cambridge University Press.

North, D.C. 1990. *Institutions, Institutional Change and Economic Performance*. Cambridg: Cambridge University Press.

Porter, M.E. 2008. *Competitive Strategy: Techniques for Analyzing Industries and Competitors.* New York: Simon & Schuster.

Rosenberg, H. 1983. *The de-Definition of Art.* Chicago: University of Chicago Press.

Saemi, S.R. 2017. "Interview by Javad Toosi." *Art & Experience Cinema.*

Schumpeter, J.A. 1934. *The Theory of Economic Development: An Inquiry into Profits, Capital, Credit, Interest, and the Business Cycle.* New Brunswick: Transaction Publishers.

Schumpeter, J. 2003. "The Theory of Economic Development: The Economy as a Whole." In *Entrepreneurship, Style and Vision*, ed. J.G. Backhaus, 61–116. Springer.

Seven. 2017. میزگرد بررسی سی و پنجمین جشنواره فجر با صندلی خالی داوران. February 10. https://telegram.me/Haft_tv3 (accessed June 10, 2017).

Stolworthy, J. 2017. *Twin Peaks Creator David Lynch Says He'll Never Make Another Film Again.* May 6. http://independent.co.uk/arts-entertainment/films/news/david-lynch-twin-peaks-return-release-date-trailer-never-directing-again-inland-empire-a7721206.html (accessed June 10, 2017).

Walsh, J. 1995. "Managerial and Organizational Cognition: Notes from a Trip Down Memory Lane." *Organization Science* 6, no. 3, pp. 280–321.

Yanal, R.J. 1998. "The Institutional Theory of Art." In *The Encyclopedia of Aesthetics*, ed. M. Kelly, 167–84. Oxford: Oxford University Press.

CHAPTER 2

We Are Not a Commercial Firm

Deirdre McQuillan

People who waffle on the question of whether or not business is an art still concede that art is, for sure, business. It has to be managed and organized to reach an audience and have an effect on it. Some artists are so good at this 'management' thing that business becomes envious and covets the secrets behind the 'art firms'.

—(Guillet de Monthoux 2005)

"We are not a commercial firm" was the response by a multi-award winning architect of international renown when asked how he would characterize his business. At the time of offering this statement his firm was active in business for 45 years with an enviable client base of individuals cited on "top 100" rich lists. Intriguingly within the arts, admitting to being "commercial" can feel uncomfortable and somehow distorted from artistic integrity. What the ordinary individual would understand as "commercial" being connected to such notions as being profitable, sustainable, or successful feels like a "sell-out" for many artists, possibly disjointed from their artistic sensibilities. Even within the artistic professions such as architecture individuals study for years to become experts in their field, but identifying with such *shameful* business practices as marketing, selling, or making a profit somehow runs counterintuitive to how they would like to be known and perceived by others.

To illuminate this problem, it is probably unhelpful to engage in explicating the simplistic differences between more mainstream traditional firms and artistic enterprises. A more subtle exploration of the paradox that exists between artists and entrepreneurship is warranted and an insight into the challenges for commercialization in the arts can provide a more useful focus to explain this reluctance by entrepreneurs to be perceived as commercial.

The Paradox of the Artist and the Entrepreneur— An Artist's Story

Tension between the artist and the entrepreneur can be interpreted as existing at the two levels. The first at the level of the individual artist and the second at the level of the workplace. There is a longstanding cultural narrative among artists of "bohemia" to justify their marginal economic position. Individuals accept a marginal economic position in order to justify their existence (Lloyd 2010). This narrative suggests a "charismatic myth" for young artists that they are called "artists" because of their extraordinary talents (Bain 2005). Artistic work, for those that connect to this story, is a calling. This "otherness" of artists also extends to a public image of the artist and his or her anti-social personality traits (Csikszentimalyi 1990; Kosmala 2007). A personality profile well described in writers, artists, and composers might be envisaged in the intensity and moodiness of Vincent van Gogh or the turbulence that existed in the marriage of Ted Hughes and Sylvia Plath. In the extreme case, this artistic personality borders on mental illness. What is missing in that analogy however is the neglect to explain how togetherness exists, or a more collective and commercially orientated conception of art and practice. Yet, this tale of individual desire often creates a self-fulfilling dynamic (Becker 2001) which may become a "tug of war" with contemporary professional dispositions required by artists for work such as political acumen, sociability, and professionalism.

In practice, starting a business, or aiming to commercialize, implies distinguishing between work and other aspects of life. There is an intrinsic relationship between the self, creative self-realization, and the work place. This introduces the second tension identified as creating a need for the special management of spaces (Kosmala 2007). The artist may require occupational solitude to create work, but for commercialization purposes that should not detract from the focus of getting paid. Problems arise however because readymade stories of the self by artists provide identification through transgression of the home-work boundaries (Bain 2005). These readymade stories also become a mode of engagement with the outside world (Kosmala 2007).

It could be suggested therefore, that many do themselves a disservice in their characterizations and self-fulfilling beliefs about who they should be as artists and how they should practice and engage with others in ways that can run counter to an entrepreneurial mindset. This paradox is perpetuated by the formation of the artist's characteristics as a dynamic between self-shaping and passive social determination implying that it may be difficult therefore to interpret the political, private, and artistic threads separately in the artist and the management of their practice (Kosmala 2007). This convolution ensures that traits normally associated with commercialism remain hidden or weak within the identity shaping behaviors of the artist.

Why is this a problem? It is a problem for entrepreneurship, because the personality of the artist reinforces the idea that they exhibit attributes of challenge, arrogance, societal interference, and hostility (Csikszentimalyi 1990; Kosmala 2007). If translated into a rebellious nature against established norms it creates challenges for organizing and working together. Entrepreneurs in the arts must recognize their need to navigate disparate domains. They must simultaneously demonstrate specialization and generalist skills, autonomy and social engagement, periphery and core location choices, artistic imaginations with commercial tasks (Lingo and Tepper 2015). But challenging assumptions and possibly desires of disconnect and an artistic lifestyle conflicts with the economics and behaviors of successful business. Quite likely however, a strong artistic identity is needed to handle the high risk and failure inherent in the sector (Bridgstock 2011; Hall 2004; Inkson 2006). Nevertheless, doing business in this challenging field requires artists to unify the paradoxical constructs and long held beliefs that normally create disjoint between the individual and his or her ability to commercialize their work.

The "Real" Challenge of Commercialism in the Arts

The artistic labor market is characterized by permanent excess supply (Bille et al. 2013) for a number of possible reasons. One reason connects to the existence of a "superstar" market (Rosen 1981) wherein relatively small numbers of people earn enormous amounts of money and dominate their segment of the arts. This seems to be increasingly important in the modern world. Sklair (2005, 2006) shows how this phenomenon has, in more recent years, evolved to become more defined and sponsored by corporate institutions and their agents. Attracted by this visible potential, many artists persist in the industry fed on the dream of superstardom and its latent rewards contributing in reality to a rather precarious existence.

Individual artists legitimize this precarious existence through reputation building and persistence despite daunting personal and professional challenges (Grazian 2004; Lena and Pachucki 2013; Lloyd 2010). Art work connects to the relative irrationality of artists (Towse 2006) who tend to engage in high uncertainty strategies or simply an irrational "work preference" to be active in the art market (Bille, Loyland, and Fjaellegaard 2012; Steiner and Schnieder 2013; Bille et al. 2013). Structurally, artists and arts-related workers face low barriers to entry and a resultant chronic underestimation of the risk involved and the chances of success (Alper and Wassall 2006; Menger 2001; Neff, Wissinger, and Zukin 2005; Throsby 1992).

Apart from the structural challenges, institutional factors are also highly influential on the work climate for artists. Government support for creative industries, creative cities (Florida 2007, 2002), and smaller enclaves (Markusen 2013) creates financing and visualization opportunities for professional artists. Conversely political censorship for example, within past communist regimes (Kosmala 2007) influences a different trajectory. Some professional artists may choose to locate their practice outside of mainstream ideology in a counter-cultural space (Andreas 1999), where underground movements challenge regimes by questioning the role of dominant systems in the construction of identity and difference (Polit 2000). Indeed, identification with the mainstream through formal art practice, state commissioning or corporate sponsorship may be frowned upon by peers, infringing on the commercialization potential of the artist seeking the respect of their community.

Between the characteristics of a somewhat irrational individual and the institutional work climate belies a fundamental challenge of commercialization in the arts. Innovation and creativity in the arts seems to rest on criticism. Caring about peers and positioning may be necessary for creativity. Peers give industry awards, publicize "good work" and often act as expert interpreters for customers or the general public. While in other playing fields innovation may rest in technology or design, the artist depends on criticism for their creativity and this requires engaging with multiple possibly disparate audiences.

Responding to this great idealism and uncertainty, artistic entrepreneurs and organizations correspondingly manage through engagement in project-based work and flexible employment (Storey, Salaman, and Platman 2005). The commercialization of organizations within the arts means dealing with businesses that sit at the crossroads of the arts, business, and technology. Entrepreneurs are trading in both business and creativity and often have particular issues when positioning their firms between satisfying clients and satisfying peers (Winch and Schneider 1993; Gutman 1988). Indeed their ambitions may involve simultaneous ambitions of satisfying clients, satisfying peers, educating and providing a social service (Rabkin 2013; Simonds 2013; Gutman 1988). Basic strategy thinking about market positioning and being "stuck in the middle" (Porter 1985) would allude to the fundamental challenges that entrepreneurs in the arts are confronted with. By trying to target multiple audiences with different needs, artists seeking to commercialize must adopt a somewhat schizophrenic visioning process.

It could also be noted that education within artistic segments plays an important role in commercialization activities. Education ultimately influences the business model of the artist itself (Moureau and Sagot-Duvauroux 2012). Characteristics of the training and early career experiences create an imprint on the artist. The Bauhaus for example was the most influential modernist art school of the 20th century, boasting a renowned faculty of artists which included Wassily Kandinsky, Josef Albers, Laszlo Moholy-Nagy, Paul Klee, and Johannes Itten architects Walter Gropius and Ludwig Mies van der Rohe, and designer Marcel Breuer. Through its artists, the Bauhaus approach to teaching and understanding art's relationship to society and technology had a major impact both in Europe and the United States long after it closed.

But what about learning commercial skills? Many arts institutions continue to emphasize disciplinary specific skill development (Lingo and Tepper 2015) despite much argument toward generalization, flexibility and broad competency skills (Iyengar 2013) required for the protean careers of artists in their challenging environment (Hall 2004; Inkson 2006). Success increasingly requires meta-competencies (Bain and McLean 2013; Bridgstock 2011) beyond the traditional disciplinary specific training of professional artists although educational institutions have been poor to respond to this need in practice.

Aside from the influence on the artist as students, recent studies have found that artists often seek to be socially engaged with their communities and perceive their role more than just an artist, but as educators and social service providers (Rabkin 2013; Simonds 2013). An additional challenge that prevents artists from developing managerial and commercial competencies is their tendency to engage in multiple job holding as a means to supplement income (Throsby and Zednik 2011; Lingo and Tepper 2015). Apart from teaching, such work is often unskilled "between jobs" work. Greater casualization in more recent years suggests more "portfolio careers" are common among artists (Throsby and Zednik 2011; Bridgstock 2005) which might facilitate the transfer of artistic skills to other domains applying creative skills in new and imaginative ways, but it is unclear how this transfers other skills back into the artistic profession. Funding from other organizational settings means that artists may fall through the cracks that are set up to support paid work in the arts (Lingo and Tepper 2015; Brown and Tepper 2012).

Thus, it is suggested that a reluctance combined with multiple structural barriers to developing commercial business skills becomes a problem for the artist insofar as he or she can end up distracted with other work. It is also a problem for the development of entrepreneurship in the field. As long as artists are not developing commercial acumen, they are unskilled in seeking and developing support that can help them to identify and engage with entrepreneurial opportunities.

Being a Sellout?

Current studies appear to suggest that the "art for art's sake" outlook (Bourdieu 1993; Lloyd 2010) traditionally affording the artist status in the field by the public and profession has evolved and many studies indicate that most artists now have little concern about selling out (Lindeman and Tepper 2012; Lingo and Tepper 2015). It is unlikely however that this is the reality for a great many individuals or indeed whether such a position is sustainable in terms of a productive and fulfilling career for many artists. Certainly there is a large trend toward replication, and this can give artists status and popularity (Lena and Pachucki 2013). This is evidenced in the music industry whereby very little original work reaches the mainstream radio charts. Boybands and girlbands proliferate the television screens in shows such as *"American Idol"* and similar examples exist across artistic segments.

For the original artist, intuitively being able to work in their field also has wide benefits for the artists themselves, for their beneficiaries and for society as a whole. However, in confronting the complexities of a commercial organization within artistic fields, entrepreneurs are also dealing with themselves and their own peculiarities. Entrepreneurs are typically thought of (somewhat mythically) as hardnosed extroverts chasing the elusive pot of gold at the end of the rainbow. But why would individuals owning creative talent and possibly after years of study not expect to sustain themselves commercially through their work. These individuals must be challenged by the creative and destructive possibilities in the process of both identity construction and business management (Jeffcut 1993). Artists demanding authorship over their output may be adverse to the interference of others, for example through marketing, client interaction, or planning but maintaining artistic integrity while confronting commercialization challenges of the field should not require selling out.

The Secrets Behind the Commercial-Uncommercial Firm

This chapter concludes by discussing what the firm that is "not a commercial firm" does well that creates commercial success. In essence maintaining the credibility of not being a commercial firm and being a commercial firm simultaneously requires success to come from creative competencies. Obviously this has restrictions on **size** because managing larger firms becomes somewhat like a bus conductor where artistic competencies are replaced by the need to manage people and teams and sheer volumes of work.

The successful commercial-uncommercial firm fosters the **image** of the artist working from the **space** of the studio environment and does not compromise on style. This means seeking **good customers** who do not interfere with the work of the artist. This is what categorizes a good customer in the commercial-uncommercial firm. Over time, good customers allow the artist to maintain their artistic integrity ensuring that their work gets seen by others and networks of relationships and appreciators build up over time. This is of course aided by **networks** in the professional sphere that may award or publicize work improving reputation and notoriety.

Technology today allows firms to promote their work and exist in spaces what would have previously ensured they remain unknown and uncommercial. The influence of technology means that physical spaces have altered and trends such as remote working and more "freelancing" that can create greater social isolation and a breakdown of traditional occupational communities (Hesmondlalgh and Baker 2010). Thus, processes for organizing are also evolving to support, advocate and connect artists to their customers and to the wider society.

Above all however, maintaining a **passion** for work makes the uncommercial commercial and ensures survival of the artist as the opening example illuminates. It is worth noting that both art and entrepreneurship calls for passion-driven action. The paradoxical commonality between a type of desire for the constant re-creation of the self into art and the absolute exertion of self into business (Pitsis 2009; Guillet de Monthoux 2005) can be answered though an unwavering passion, an unwillingness to compromise on work and a **business model** that reflects these values.

References

Alper, N., and G. Wassall. 2006. "Artist's careers and their labour markets." *Handbook of the Economics of Art and Culture* 1, pp. 813–64.

Andreas, E. 1999. "Gender Minefield, the Heritage of the Past." *International Feminist Art Journal* 11, pp. 4–9.

Bain, A. 2005. "Constructing an Artistic Identity." *Work, Employment and Society* 19, no. 1, pp. 25–46.

Bain, A., and D. McLean. 2013. "From Post to Poster to Post-Industrialist: Cultural Networks and Eclectic Creative Practice." In *Cultural Economies in Post-Industrial Cities: Manufacturing a (Different) Scene*, ed. M. Breitbart. Aldershot: Ashgate.

Becker, G. 2001. "The Association of Creativity and Psychopathology: Its Cultural Historial Origins." *Creativity Research Journal* 13, pp. 45–53.

Bille, T., C. Bryld Fjaellegaard, B. Frey, and L. Steiner. 2013. "Happiness in the Arts—Internationla Evidence on Artists' Job Satisfaction." *Economic Letters* 121, pp. 15–18.

Bille, T., K. Loyland, and C. Fjaellegaard. 2012. "Work for Passion—Labour Supply of Norwegian Artists." 17th International Conference on Cultural Economics, Kyoto, Japan.

Bourdieu, P. 1993. *The Field of Cultural Production: Essays on Art and Literature.* New York: Columbia University Press.

Bridgstock, R. 2005. "Australian Artists, Starving and Well-Nourished: What Can We Learn from the Prototypical Protean Career?" *Australian Journal of Career Development* 14, pp. 40–47.

Bridgstock, R. 2011. "Skills for Creative Industries Graduate Success." *Education and Training* 53, no. 1, pp. 9–26.

Brown, A., and S. Tepper. 2012. *Placing the Arts at the Heart of the Creative Campus.* New York: Association of Performing Arts Presenters.

Csikszentimalyi, M. 1990. "The Domain of Creativity." In *Theories of Creativity*, eds. M. Runco and R. Albert. Newbury Park, CA: Sage.

Florida, R. 2002. *The Rise of the Creative Class: and How it's Transforming Work, Leisure, Community, and Everyday Life.* New York: Basic Books.

Florida, R. 2007. *The Flight of the Creative Class: The New Global Competition for Talent.* New York: HarperCollins.

Grazian, D. 2004. "Production of Popular Music as Confidence Games." *Qualitative Sociology* 27, pp. 137–258.

Guillet de Monthoux, P. 2005. "Momo Management: A Note on the Insultant Antonin Artaud and his Clients." *Culture and Organization* 11, no. 4, pp. 259–68.

Gutman, R. 1988. *Architectural Practice: A Critical Review.* New York: Princeton Architectural Press.

Hall, D. 2004. "The Protean Career: A Quarter-Century Journey." *Journal of Vocational Behaviour* 65, no. 1, pp. 1–13.

Hesmondlalgh, D., and S. Baker. 2010. "A Very Complicated Version of Freedom: Conditions and Experiences of Creative Labour in Three Cultural Industries." *Poetics* 38, pp. 4–20.

Inkson, K. 2006. "Protean and Boundaryless Careers as Methphors." *Journal of Vocational Behaviour* 69, pp. 48–63.

Iyengar, S. 2013. "Artists by the Numbers: Moving from Descriptive Statistics to Impact Analyses." *Work and Occupations* 40, pp. 496–505.

Jeffcut, P. 1993. "From Interpretation to Representation." In *Postmodernism and Organizations*, eds. J. Hassard and M. Parker. London: Sage.

Kosmala, K. 2007. "The Identity Paradox? Reflections on Fluid Identity of Female Artist." *Culture and Organization* 13, no. 1, pp. 37–53.

Lena, J., and M. Pachucki. 2013. "The Sincerest Form of Flattery; Innovation, Repetition and Status in the Art Movement." *Poetics* 41, pp. 236–64.

Lindeman, D., and S. Tepper. 2012. *Painting with Broader Strokes: Reassessing the Value of an Arts Degree*. Indiana: University of Indiana.

Lingo, E., and S. Tepper. 2015. "Looking Back, Looking Forward: Arts-Based Careers and Creative Work." *Work and Occupations* 40, no. 4, pp. 337–63.

Lloyd, R. 2010. *Neo-Bohemia: Art and Commerce in the Postindustiral City*. New York: Routledge.

Markusen, A. 2013. "Artists Work Everywhere." *Work and Occupations* 40, no. 4, pp. 481–95.

Menger, P. 2001. "Artists as Workers: Theoretical and Methodological Challenges." *Poetics* 28, pp. 241–54.

Moureau, N., and D. Sagot-Duvauroux. 2012. "Four Business Models in Contemporary Art." *International Journal of Arts Management* 14, no. 3, pp. 44–56.

Neff, G., E. Wissinger, and S. Zukin. 2005. "Entrepreneurial Labour Among Cultural Producers: 'Cool' Jobs in 'hot' Industries." *Social Semiotics* 15, pp. 307–34.

Pitsis, A. 2009. "Artaud's Poetic Vision and Some Comments on Frederick Taylor." *Advances in Organization Studies* 4, pp. 67–81.

Polit, P. 2000. Experiences of Discourse: Polish Art of 1965–1975. In *ARTMargins*.

Porter, M. 1985. "Competitive Strategy." In *Competitive Advantage: Creating and Sustaining Superior Performance*. New York: Free Press, Simon and Schuster Adult Publishing Group.

Rabkin, N. 2013. "Teaching Artists: A Century of Tradition and a Commitment to Change." *Work and Occupations* 40, pp. 506–13.

Rosen, S. 1981. "The Economics of Superstars." *American Economic Review* 71, pp. 845–58.

Simonds, W. 2013. "Presidential Address: The Art of Activism." *Social Problems* 60, no. 1, pp. 1–26.

Sklair, L. 2005. "The Transnational Capitalist Class and Contemporary Architecture in Globalizing Cities." *International Journal of Urban and Regional Research* 29, no. 3, pp. 485–500.

Sklair, L. 2006. "Iconic Architecture and Capitalist Globalization." *City* 10, no. 1, pp. 22–47.

Steiner, L., and L. Schnieder. 2013. "The Happy Artist? An Empirical Application of the Work-Preference Model." *Journal of Cultural Economics* 37, pp. 225–46.

Storey, J., G. Salaman, and K. Platman. 2005. "Living with Enterprise in an Entreprise Economy: Freelance and Contract Workers in the Media." *Human Relations* 58, pp. 1033–54.

Throsby, D. 1992. "Artists as Workers." In *Cultural Economics*, eds. R. Towse and A. Khakee, 201–08. Berlin: Springer.

Throsby, D., and A. Zednik. 2011. "Multiple Job-Holdingand Artistic Careers: Some Empirical Evidence." *Cultural Trends* 20, no. 1, pp. 9–24.

Towse, R. 2006. "Human Capital and Artists' Labour Markets." In *Handbook of Economics of Art and Culture*, eds. A. Victor and T. David, 865–94. Elsevier.

Winch, G., and E. Schneider. 1993. "Managing the Knowledge-Based Organization: The Case of Architectural Practice." *Journal of Management Studies* 30, no. 6, pp. 923–37.

CHAPTER 3

Creating Value in the Performing Arts Industries: A Process for Arts Entrepreneurs

Sara Theis and Mark C. Samples

Introduction

This chapter presents a complete process for designing and creating value in a performing arts industry context, from idea-generation to the point where the project is ready to launch. This means that the process focuses on the foundational stages of a project, its inception and early development, rather than later stages such as promotion, pricing, and technical execution of the performance, product, or service. By focusing on creating value early, artist entrepreneurs can develop a stronger position for their project when they transition from project design to project execution. Some scholarship has been accomplished with regard to the public and intrinsic benefits of the arts, such as McCarthy et al. (2004). Yet a study of the particular processes for creating those benefits, and the specific challenges faced by artist entrepreneurs is lacking. This chapter seeks to begin filling this gap.

Drawing on the authors' experiences and research, the chapter is organized around the recommended phases that any artist entrepreneur go through in the beginning stages of a venture. Each phase is designed to ensure that value is created for customers.

1. Clarifying Artistic Philosophy
2. Idea Generation

3. Visioning

4. Developing a Customer Profile

5. Goal Setting and Strategies for Execution

6. Defining a Business Structure

7. The Premortem

8. Reflect, Revise, Repeat

Examples in this chapter will be drawn from the fields of theater and of music, since those are the authors' fields of expertise. But the principles and strategies proposed here apply more broadly to entrepreneurs in other artistic domains. In this chapter, the term "artist entrepreneur" has been chosen to refer to this broad and varied set of practitioners, including actors, directors, musicians, composers, and dancers, as well as arts administrators and others.

Following the phases described in this chapter does not guarantee success, for developing a sustainable career in the arts presents many challenges. As emphasized in the following, success requires obtaining constant input from prospective customers, continual analysis of market characteristics, and a willingness to adjust one's value proposition and mode of delivery when required. It is hoped, however, that explaining these phases and suggesting an order for working through them will provide a model for artist entrepreneurs to develop the skill of identifying, honing, and creating value in their communities.

Clarifying Artistic Philosophy

A crucial difference between entrepreneurs and *artist entrepreneurs* is that the latter typically have domain-specific skills that guide their choice of industry. Whereas an entrepreneur might search for a need in various markets and choose the most profitable opportunity in the most feasible market, an artist entrepreneur's search is more focused. A musician with skills in composition and conducting, for example, might consider starting a community orchestra or becoming a film music composer, but she likely would not consider the more classic entrepreneurial options, such as franchising a restaurant or starting a t-shirt business. In addition to opportunities for profit, artists seek outlets that will resonate with their personal artistic values. It is a deeply ingrained belief in artist-communities that there is a difference between successful artists who are true to their core artistic values, and those who "sell out." By building an authentic personal brand, the performing artist can more clearly pursue a version of himself and his art that promotes natural strengths (Radbill 2017, 96). The goal of an artist entrepreneur therefore is to create a career that is not only financially sustainable, but also artistically fulfilling.

In planning a venture or a career, artist-entrepreneurs must first discover and define their own core artistic values, a concept that can be called one's artistic philosophy, or in business terms, their "brand values." Brand values, in this case, refer to the core characteristics of a business. They include not only the basic characteristics of a business's identity, but also outline how a business distinguishes itself in the marketplace. Brand values link a brand to products and broader concepts, such as peak athletic performance (Nike) or beautifully simple technology (Apple; Jones 2017). These brand values then become a rubric by which to evaluate business opportunities and assess a project's success.

A good place to start when discovering one's brand values is to first look back (Reflection), then look forward (Forecasting). First, the artist entrepreneur should reflect on her past activities and search for broader patterns that emerge. Begin by asking the following reflective questions: "What am I most passionate about?" "What do other people come to me for?" "What activities make me lose track of time?" The performing artist can also ask close colleagues to answer the same questions, as sometimes others can see patterns that are invisible to the artist. The exercise of reflection should continue with broader questions: "Which of my artistic activities have led to the most personal, social, and cultural fulfillment?" After reflecting on past successes, she should spend time forecasting future activities through an idealized lens: "If I could design an ideal performance, what would it look like?" "What do my ideal audience members look and act like?" "In 10 years, what activities and projects would I have to be working on to feel artistically fulfilled?" When approaching these questions, be as specific as possible, giving concrete and detailed answers. Also, be sure to record answers either on paper or through a voice recorder. At the end of this phase of Reflection and Forecasting, the artist entrepreneur should know what domain her business idea will inhabit. Just as important, she will disqualify many opportunities from her view, allowing a greater focus and creativity in the domain that matters most.

Though it may seem that an artist's domain-specificity unduly limits opportunities, it can also work as an advantage. Performing artists have typically spent years in focused skill acquisition, developing their craft to expert level. Scientific research has shown that grit (Duckworth 2016) and deliberate practice (Ericsson and Pool 2016) are skills that accompany broader success in a predictable and even causative way. Professional musicians, and other top performers who have trained extensively such as athletes and chess masters, are often studied by researchers precisely because of their ability to hone skills to a high level over time. By clarifying and writing down one's artistic philosophy, the artist entrepreneur can leverage the thousands of hours of focused skill development into a business that creates value for others.

Idea Generation

Once the artist entrepreneur has clarified an artistic philosophy, the next step is to generate an idea that will contribute value. In order to do this, it is important to begin considering potential customers. Early consideration of who the customer is will help to focus the business idea, and a full customer profile will be described in full later in this chapter. "Customers," for this purpose, is a broad term meaning those who will take advantage of the product or offering. Customers could be people who buy tickets to a performance or people who will use a product or service or people who will contract the artist to do work for their existing business or people who will benefit in some way by the offer. Ideas may exist about how customers may view the particular solution to their problem, but until meaningful discussion is had to gain feedback, the ideas are only guesses. There are many ways ideas can be strengthened to create more value for the customer. Based on the feedback, make appropriate adjustments to the product or service. Revise, revise, revise. The fact of the matter is, unless someone else, a customer, sees value in the art and is willing and able to engage in it, it is not a business or a career path. Other people, customers, are the key to success for the artist entrepreneur.

Step two in this process is coming up with a business idea. The idea of creating a business can be scary for artists, because so many of the concepts seem foreign. There are numbers involved, and they are not "five, six, seven, eight." Later in the chapter, the business model canvas will be discussed to help think through what is required when creating an arts-based business. Each business has a model. It may be simple like baking cookies in the kitchen and selling them to the entrepreneur's own family and friends or it could be very complex like the federal government.

There are a couple of tools that can help generate better ideas. The first is a game of "What's Missing?" the authors' variation of the common practice of looking at the competitive landscape in a given market and searching for opportunities in the gaps. This works well for artist entrepreneurs who want to engage a specific community in the arts in some way. Make a list of all of the arts-based businesses within a specific market, figure out what is not there, and pursue the most feasible opportunities in the gap. This is called opportunity recognition, an important skill for entrepreneurs seeking to create value in their industry. In an ideal world, this is a community need, and it is a business idea that has a higher probability of succeeding because it is entirely missing. A conversation with the customer base is in order at this point in time. It is possible that the particular artform does not exist within a community because there is no interest. If there is no interest or engagement in that artform, a new business will likely fail without cultivation. At this point, the artist entrepreneur should begin to examine if there is a path to cultivating interest or engagement in the offer.

The "What's Missing?" activity was done with a group of students recently. The idea was to create an arts-based business located in Decatur, Illinois. Each student compiled a list of the arts programming and businesses in and adjacent to this city and, surprisingly, there are quite a few in this urban of 80,000 people. One student identified synchronized swimming as an artform that was entirely absent from the city's arts landscape. The student dutifully completed his business model canvas and created programming that would support teaching students to swim before entering classes that would ultimately train them to be a member of a synchronized swimming team. The training was similar to what one might see in a dance studio sequence, with the instructor teaching basic skills to younger students and more artful execution to students with advanced experience. The student's idea needed a little more investigation before it could progress. He was asked to explore what the offerings were for swim lessons, an adjacent industry offering. He discovered a landscape riddled with options. In Decatur, Illinois, one can engage in swim lessons through the local park district, the YMCA, several day care centers around the area, and high schools. Moreover, an interested student could take private lessons through multiple area teachers. Each company offers options for multiple age ranges and skill levels. Swimming is alive and well in this community. There is an argument to be made that this market is saturated and there would be no way to create a successful business in this realm. The student's market research led to an important adjustment to the model. Instead of entering the market as a competitor, he chose to make the people engaging in those offerings his target market and his programming would be adjusted to build on the skills that they learned through these existing programs. He identified those organizations as potential partners rather than competitors and was able to scale back his own programming needs to focus on building engagement with synchronized swimming specifically. This type of arrangement is called "synergy" (Byrnes 2015).

The second tool for generating ideas comes from design thinking practices and is for brainstorming problems with a specific event or process in mind. This process works best with a group of people with some working knowledge of the question at hand. Give each member of the group a stack of sticky notes and pose a broad question like, "What are all of the problems with theater?" or "What are all of the problems with rehearsal?" Ask each member of the group to list one problem per sticky note (quantity over quality), and give them a limited amount of time (about three minutes) to come up with as many problems as possible. Next, group similar responses together, discuss similarities, identify root/core problems, and create possible ideas for solutions. Next, set to work understanding the problem's ideal outcome. The problem can be highly complex, such as "arts organizations lack diversity," or fairly simple, such as "the stage floor takes a long time to dry after mopping."

Once the problem has been clearly identified, state it succinctly and move into the next step of the process. This step or the previous one can be revisited as necessary. Remember, arts entrepreneurship is a process and bouncing back and forth between steps to clarify or change any part of it is not only suggested but also required in order to reach a sustainable arts business idea.

Visioning

Visioning is the next step in the process of developing an arts business that creates value. "Visioning" is imagining what the world looks like if the venture is successful in fulfilling its mission. There are internal and external components of this process, and both are essential. Artist entrepreneurs need to define for themselves what they believe success looks like, and then, test their assumptions within their customer base.

During the internal part of process, ask "What does success in this endeavor look like? Who are the people impacted? What are they doing? How do I know success is achieved?" Find a visual way of representing the answers. It could be drawing, collage or any other medium. It is important to clarify what success looks like or how the world is impacted because of this business. That will determine what steps are taken to impact the problem. At this point in the process, the broad impact of the arts-based business is what is being considered. The artist entrepreneur can spend time drilling down on specific metrics to achieve later. This information will become the "vision" statement for the organization, which differs from a mission statement in a critical way. A mission defines the organization's purpose and for whom. A vision statement defines what the impact will be on the world because this organization exists (Rosewell 2014).

For example, suppose the issue being addressed is "arts organizations lack diversity." That is a very broad problem to solve and it is incredibly complex. Suppose that, based on the artistic philosophy developed earlier, this artist entrepreneur has identified a philosophy grounded in acting and a love of elementary school children. The outcome that is drawn may be as simple as more members of underrepresented communities in leadership positions of existing organizations. The way that one might approach this goal is to create a program that follows specific students and creates resources and opportunities over time that allow them to be better prepared to take on leadership positions. Alternatively, the vision might be to have large audiences composed of members of underrepresented communities. The way that one might approach this vision is programming aimed at engaging those community members early to develop a love of the arts and, in turn, create their own arts organizations. For both outcomes, the artist entrepreneur's artistic philosophy is intact.

Once the internal test has been completed, the artist entrepreneur must test her ideas externally by talking to potential customers. The focus group of customers that was identified needs to be engaged in a conversation to gain a better understanding of the issue at hand. The goal is to get to the heart of the problem. What is the big headache? For example, if the discussion about slow-drying stage floors is being had with stagehands, a discovery may be made that a new fast-drying mop solution is required to solve the issue. Alternately, the discovery may be that there is too much stuff on the stage when mopping begins. Drying might take a long time because the stagehands have to stop every 30 seconds to move something and it would be better if the stage were cleared the night before. The solution to the latter is a process improvement aimed at benefitting this specific group. No matter how amazing a new mop product is, it will not solve a process issue. This new understanding of the problem would not come about without listening to and absorbing what the customers say. As a result, the team can make whatever adjustments are necessary to better serve the customer base.

Beyond internal and external tests, another tool that can be used to clarify a business's vision is an exercise called "Headlines" (Allison 2005, 104–105). Imagine it is 10 years in the future and the organization has just made the national news. Write a headline to describe what that is. *Acme Corporation sells One Trillion Mops* is quite different from *Five-Minute Preset: A New Standard for Live Performance*. If the goal is selling one trillion mops, an expansion of the customer base is necessary to hit that mark. If the goal is a five-minute preset, mopping is not the only process that will need to be addressed.

Developing a Customer Profile

Knowing one's customer is crucial to refining a vision into one that will ultimately provide value. The big hindrance here is that entrepreneurs typically think they already know their customers, but are often mistaken. All entrepreneurs struggle with this, but artists have an extra barrier. There is a long-standing cultural belief that artists should only think of themselves, and changing one's art because of customer need or desire is a form of selling out. This, however, is a historical and cultural myth harbored by amateurs, not professionals. There is a difference between compromising one's artistic values and philosophy (which is strongly advised against) and communicating one's art in a way that is valuable to others (what this chapter is about). Knowing one's customers cannot replace the work of preparing an artist's craft, but it is essential for the sustainability of an arts venture.

How does one go about knowing customers better? Ask them. Asking can take many forms, such as surveys, informal interviews with community members, or interacting with prospective customers where they congregate online. One simple way to understand a customer's perceptions of value is to simply ask two questions: (1) "What are your greatest fears or frustrations?" and (2) "What are your greatest hopes or desires?" (Be sure to limit the domain of the question to the issue that is under investigation.) Beyond this, one should complete a thorough customer profile in the beginning stages of any major project. A customer profile, if accurate, will provide a lighthouse reference for deciding what elements of one's art will ultimately be delivered to customers, and how it will be delivered.

Another useful approach to a building a strong customer profile was developed by Osterwalder et al. (2014). Readers are advised to refer to the full resource, but a summary of the steps here will provide a start. First, define the business's customer segments. In the case of a violin teaching studio, for instance, the two main customer segments might be the young students as well as their parents. Next, collect what Osterwalder and Pigneur call "customer jobs." These refer to the tasks that customers want to get done. In the case of the parents of a violin student, customer jobs might include anything from wanting child care for an hour to wanting to give their child a well-balanced life. Finally, make separate, ranked lists of "pains" (pain points with regard to the customer jobs) and "gains" (desired benefits to the customer with regard to customer jobs) that each customer segment feels.

The first draft of a customer profile will likely be completed internally, but the real power of a customer profile comes when it has been tested against real prospective customers and refined in an iterative way.

Goal Setting and Strategies for Execution

Based on the developed customer profile and vision, it is time to begin to further define what success means and how the artist entrepreneur determines that it is achieved. One of the great things about arts-based businesses is that the artist is the one who decides what metrics will be used to measure success. The concept of clarity in goal setting has been around at least since Peter Drucker's classic guide, *The Practice of Management*, was first published in 1954. The objective in whatever method is chosen to construct goals is to make them clearly accomplishable. They should be defined in a way that allows clarity to know when they are done. This is the difference between "get work out there" and "integrate arts education programming aimed at engaging underrepresented communities into three schools in urban Chicago within two years."

A strategy for execution is the means to an end. That is to say, it is the way that one will go about achieving a goal. There are a lot of factors at play in determining a strategy. The first step is to engage in a self-study of sorts. What are the tools the artist entrepreneur, herself, brings to the table? Entrepreneurship professor Heidi Neck, in a keynote address at the 2016 Society for Arts Entrepreneurship Education in Decatur, Illinois, offered a series of questions to uncover one's strengths in this regard. "Who am I? What do I have? Who do I know? What can I do today, this week, this month?" Answering these questions helps to develop strategies of execution that match with an individual's skill set and experience.

The next step is to get feedback once again from the identified customer base. The proposed goals and strategies need to be measured against the problem that has been identified. To this end, Alex Bruton of the Straight Up Business Institute offers *The Critique Pad*, a valuable tool that measures the impact and feasibility of a business idea (www.straightupbusiness.institute/toolkit). To assess an idea, ask customers to rate the proposed solution with regard to impact and feasibility, each on a scale from 1 to 10. Impact answers the question, "Will the proposed solution fix the identified problem?" Feasibility answers, "Can the proposed solution be delivered?" Combine the two scores to get an overall impact and feasibility score: high value can be obtained with high scores on both questions. This rating should come from the customer because the customer is the one who will ultimately decide the value of the product or service offered. If one or the other is lacking, make the necessary revisions and try again.

Defining a Business Structure

Once a value proposition has been developed and tested and the business's vision and brand values have been clarified, the artist entrepreneur should go to work on the structure their business will take. Should the business be structured as a non-profit, a Limited Liability Company (LLC), or another type of corporation? Will the business make one-time sales or use a membership model? What are the key revenue sources and cost structures of the business? What are the business's key resources and partners? Honing a business structure that is appropriate to the venture is critical for success, because it is the apparatus through which one can deliver value to customers and create a sustainable business. If the artist entrepreneur does not have previous training in business, this is the time to begin researching what resources are available, including industry business and legal guides (e.g., Hearn 2017; Halloran 2017), and the chamber of commerce in the state or province where the business will be located. Although they do not address arts entrepreneurship directly, general entrepreneurship textbooks might also be useful, since they cover standard business practices such as budgeting and accounting (see for instance Kuratko 2014; Bamford and Bruton 2016)

At this point in the process, the artist entrepreneur may already have ideas about how the business should be structured, and it might be tempting to rush through this process and choose the first option that comes to mind. This would be a mistake. First, the artist entrepreneur should widen her options and seek counsel from an experienced and trusted business owner. Then, she should carefully consider how her business structure will support her in the short and long term. By taking time now to plan and define a business model, the artist entrepreneur can avoid major structural problems in the future.

There are many resources available for developing a business model, ranging from a simple brainstorming session to a complete business plan (for an example of a shorter business plan template that an artist might use, see Cutler 2010, 43–48). The most complete and approachable tool for the arts professional is the Business Model Canvas. The Business Model Canvas was developed by Alexander Osterwalder and Yves Pigneur for the purpose of clarifying an entrepreneur's understanding and relationship of the essential components of a business (Osterwalder and Pigneur 2010). With this tool, all essential components of a business can be represented on a single page. Additionally, the model is accessible to artists who have had little or no previous experience with business models or business plans. There are nine categories, described as follows. A *value proposition* is a statement that communicates the value delivered to the customer. *Customer segments* refer to primary and secondary customer groups who receive value provided by the product or service. *Customer relationships* define the nature of the business's relationship with customers, such as memberships, enrollment, or one-time sales. *Channels* are the means by which value is delivered to customers, such as store-front, classroom, or shipping. *Key Activities* refer to all important and repeating activities needed to deliver value to the customer. *Key resources* are the human, material, and knowledge resources needed to deliver value to the customer. *Key Partners* are the external companies and people needed to sustain the business. *Cost Structure* refers to the cost categories required to make the business structure sustainable. *Revenue streams* are the sources of revenue created by the business structure. A final crucial step is to compare the model to its surrounding marketplace environment. It is important to consider what other businesses are providing similar services, and develop a value proposition and model that is distinct and competitive in the local landscape.

Note that the business model canvas allows for categories to be approached in any order, and can each be updated continuously in an iterative process. Nevertheless, the authors encourage a special focus on the value proposition early on, because a clear and refined value proposition will lead to clarity in other areas of the business. Each category in the canvas can be turned into a checklist that will guide the artist entrepreneur through a complete consideration of the business's structure. Note that while these are in list form, they can be approached out of sequence given each artist entrepreneur's specific situation.

- Develop a clearly stated and refined value proposition.
- List all customer segments and rank in order of importance.
- Define primary customer relationships.
- Establish the primary channel by which value will be delivered to customers.
- List all key activities needed for success, including one-time and repeating activities.
- List all key human, material, and knowledge resources needed.
- List the critical suppliers, accrediting agencies, and other partners needed to deliver value to customers.
- List all major cost categories.
- List all sources of revenue and rank in order of priority.

Another benefit of developing a business model is that it helps the artist entrepreneur identify resources, time, money, and people that are still needed. By working through a complete business model, the artist entrepreneur will have the opportunity to resolve resource deficits early through acquisition, building a team, partnering with other businesses, or developing vendor contracts.

The Premortem

Once the initial business model and all of the previous steps are completed, the final step in the process is to conduct a "premortem" for the project. Often, arts professionals do an exercise after a venture fails, analyzing what went wrong and fixing it for next time. This is sometimes called the "postmortem." Entrepreneurs can also perform a premortem, a thought experiment that helps them identify the key points of potential failure in the project before they begin, then to design strategies to avoid those problems. The premortem concept was developed by psychologist Gary Klein and described in his book *Streetlights and Shadows: Searching for the Keys to Adaptive Decision Making* (Klein 2009). The procedure presented subsequently follows Chip and Dan Heath's detailed discussion of the practice in their book *Decisive: How to Make Better Decisions in Life and Work* (2013). Because the exercise assumes an already-defined project, it is best to do this activity in the later stages of a project's development.

Klein describes the premise of the premortem technique: "In a premortem, you ask your team to pretend that a crystal ball shows that in a few weeks or months your new venture has failed. The team members then write down all the reasons why it failed." (Klein 2009, 63). By identifying potential failure points for a venture or project, preventative measures can be put in place beforehand, increasing the ability of the entrepreneur to respond. Following is one way to perform a project premortem.

- Gather in a room with pen and paper, or a whiteboard with pens.
- 5 min.: Brainstorm the following prompt in teams of three or four: "Eight weeks from now your project was a total fiasco. It totally failed to meet the requirements of the project, and did not achieve the desired results. Why did it fail? List twenty reasons."
- 10 min.: Share with entire group the reasons, recording them on a piece of paper or whiteboard. Include tick marks for doubles.
- 15 min.: Determine the top for potential reasons for failure, and develop solutions for each, either in teams or individually.

Use the solutions created in the premortem process to either update the Business Model Canvas designed earlier, or as contingency plans during the execution of the project. By taking the time to identify potential pitfalls before the project begins, artist entrepreneurs can proactively prepare to respond to a wide variety challenges, and therefore will be more likely to succeed in creating value for their customers.

Conclusion: Reflect, Revise, Repeat

Though this chapter proposes an overall process for value creation in arts entrepreneurship, further research is needed to demonstrate the particular challenges faced by artist entrepreneurs in each phase. Moreover, each arts industry has significant differences in the way its products are produced, distributed, and consumed. A look at individual industries such as music, theater, or the visual arts through the lens of value creation would be a fruitful exercise. Nevertheless, the process introduced here aims to capture elements common across the performing and visual arts.

Approaching an arts entrepreneurship venture through the lens of value creation can make the process of launching a business more efficient and artistically fulfilling from start to finish. By following the process outlined in this chapter, an artist entrepreneur can increase the odds that her undertaking will succeed. To implement this proposed process, follow the steps subsequently listed.

1. Define and write down an artistic philosophy.
2. Generate ideas that fit within the artistic philosophy and fill a need in the artist's community.
3. Cast a vivid vision of the successful venture.
4. Develop a field-tested customer profile.
5. Take action by setting goals and strategies of execution for the venture.
6. Define a business model.
7. Conduct a premortem to identify and prepare for potential failure points.

In addition to the aforementioned steps, two overarching principles should be implemented throughout. First, test all assumptions and decisions by talking to customers. By seeking and analyzing external feedback, the artist entrepreneur can avoid the common pitfall of creating a product or service that does not have a market. Second, be open to revising business decisions when the evidence warrants it. Through reflection and data analysis, the artist entrepreneur can create an iterative development process that is responsive enough to meet the needs of customer segments but still affirms the entrepreneur's artistic philosophy.

By following the processes and applying the principles herein, more arts businesses can be created that add value to their communities, and more artist entrepreneurs can successfully design a career for themselves that is both financially sustainable and artistically fulfilling.

References

Allison, M., and J. Kaye. 2005. *Strategic Planning for Nonprofit Organizations*, 2nd ed. Hoboken, NJ: John Wiley & Sons, Inc.

Bamford, C.E., and G.D. Bruton. 2016. *Entrepreneurship: The Art, Science, and Process for Success*, 2nd ed. New York: McGraw-Hill Education.

Byrnes, W.J. 2015. *Management and the Arts*, 5th ed. Burlington, MA: Focal Press.

Cutler, D. 2010. *The Savvy Musician: Building a Career, Earning a Living, and Making a Difference*. Pittsburgh: Helius Press.

Drucker, P.F. 1993 (1954). *The Practice of Management*. New York: HarperBusiness.

Duckworth, A. 2016. *Grit: The Power of Passion and Perseverance*. New York: Scribner.

Ericsson, K.A., and R. Pool. 2016. *Peak: Secrets from the New Science of Expertise*. New York: Houghton Mifflin Harcourt.

Halloran, M. 2017. *The Musician's Business and Legal Guide*, 5th ed. New York: Routledge.

Hearn, E.R. 2017. "Business Entities." In *The Musician's Business and Legal Guide*, ed. M. Halloran, 5th ed., 10–17. New York: Routledge.

Heath, C., and D. Heath. 2013. *Decisive: How to Make Better Decisions in Life and Work*. New York: Crown Business.

Jones, R. 2017. *Branding: A Very Short Introduction*. New York: Oxford University Press.

Klein, G. 2009. *Streetlights and Shadows: Searching for the Keys to Adaptive Decision Making*. Cambridge, MA: The MIT Press.

Kuratko, D.F. 2014. *Entrepreneurship: Theory, Process, Practice*, 9th ed. Mason, OH: Cengage Learning.

McCarthy, K.F., E.H. Ondaatje, L. Zakaras, and A. Brooks. 2004. *Gifts of the Muse: Reframing the Debate about the Benefits of the Arts*. Santa Monica, CA: Rand Corporation.

Osterwalder, A., and Y. Pigneur. 2010. *Business Model Generation*. Hoboken, NJ: John Wiley & Sons, Inc.

Osterwalder, A., Y. Pigneur, G. Bernarda, and A. Smith. 2014. *Value Proposition Design*. Hoboken, NJ: John Wiley & Sons, Inc.

Radbill, C.F. 2017. *Introduction to the Music Industry: An Entrepreneurial Approach*, 2nd ed. New York: Routledge.

Rosewell, E. 2014. *Arts Management: Uniting Arts and Audiences in the 21st Century*. New York: Oxford University Press.

PART II

Arts Culture, Values and Internationalization

CHAPTER 4

Cultural Embeddedness in the Arts

Deirdre McQuillan

The Arts and Culture

Ways that artists create knowledge can intrigue all the senses through music, images, and the spoken word. Indeed art is one of the most important means of expression developed by human beings and is manifested in every aspect of life. Artists, through their creation of images or objects, have always shown a deep concern about life around them often recording in paintings, objects or music their observation of people going about their usual everyday tasks. Consider the works of the 17th century painter Johannes Vermeer who specialized in domestic interior scenes of middle-class life; or James Joyce's Ulysses, a modernist novel based on the ordinary encounters of Leopold Bloom in Dublin during the course of one ordinary day, 16th June 1904. In essence, artists and the arts more generally act as creators, interpreters, and communicators of culture conveying the totality of behavior and products of human work and thought.

Culture has been defined in hundreds of ways adhering to both its importance and to its elusive and intangible nature. Grasping culture is complicated and often problematic. Yet, it is vital to how individuals see themselves and their place in the world. By synthesizing more than 100 definitions of culture Whitely and England (1977) arrive at a working definition as "the knowledge, beliefs, art, law, morals, customs and other capabilities of one group distinguishing it from other groups." Culture creates affinity for people based on what they know. But it also creates curiosity and sometimes barriers because of society's tendency to judge their own beliefs and value systems against those of others. Although there may be divergent opinions, there is a broad consensus about the fundamental features of culture as firstly, a shared group property; secondly, a mostly intangible construct where many elements need to be inferred; and thirdly, a construct that is confirmed by others and must be observed by others from the outside (Shenkar, Luo, and Chi 2015).

Understanding how culture is defined and its fundamental features is important when artists move from satisfying their own needs to satisfying the needs of others for payment. Indeed entrepreneurship in the arts belongs to the creative or cultural segment of the economy (DCMS 1998). Entrepreneurs in cultural industries may wish to consider how they can expand out of their familiar markets and attract new customers. Alternatively, they may need to understand more tangibly how they can respond to cultural events and changes in their own cultural groupings. Cultural industries are among the most dynamic sectors of the world economy. Statistics show that in times of economic crisis the cultural industries (or interchangeably, often referred to as creative industries) can offer potentially more resilient, inclusive, and environmentally viable paths to recovery for both mature and developing nations (UNCTAD 2010; DCMS 2011). An increasing number of governments, in developing and mature countries alike, are identifying creative industries as a priority sector in their national development strategies. Growth across international boundaries is often supported by governments in a specialized manner, by setting up special agencies to promote art and culture separately from businesses. For example, the *British Council* and the German *Goethe Institute* are worldwide cultural institutes for promoting language, cultural exchange, education, and relations for their respective nations.

In understanding the elusiveness of culture however, it is not that surprising that entrepreneurs and organizations active within the creative industries (that are not technology dependent) overwhelmingly tend to remain small and local. Place plays an important role for artists maybe because of a culture rich history or a cluster effect (Scott 2006; Florida 2007), although this would appear to be devolving as the Internet, recreation and environmental preferences trump what big city clusters offer (Markusen 2013). Nevertheless, being embedded within a culture and place creates somewhat of a predicament for artists that would like to grow and make a living from their work. Certainly national level institutions may support a policy of international trade development for creative industries. However, culture is not always defined by a geographic boundary, nor do financial incentives and promotion substantially assist artist entrepreneurs in creating work that will be positively observed by others to the extent that those others are willing to pay for it. Rather, a deep understanding of what cultural embeddedness means for entrepreneurs in the arts, a knowledge of how art traverses cultures and to what extent art can aspire to be culture-free can guide artists more authentically in their creativity. Conceptualizing these ideals can provide a valuable upstream influence for entrepreneuring artists that can influence positioning and impact of their artistic work.

Some artist entrepreneurs cross cultural domains very successfully although the literature provides limited insight of how this happens. For example, in 1994 two college drop-outs Cathal Gaffney and Darragh O'Connell borrowed £2,000 and found the Irish animation company Brown Bag Films. Within its 25 years of existence the firm picked up a host of international awards including Oscar nominations, six Emmy awards and a host of BAFTA and Annie nominations for their hit shows. So while many entrepreneurial artists may feel confined to selling at local weekend markets and craft fairs, some achieve great global success providing offerings with substantial international appeal. Interpreting this phenomenon may be guided by an innate understanding of what it means to be culturally embedded or culture-free.

Cultural Embeddedness in the Arts

In nearly all regions of the world, one ethnic group predominates by sheer population numbers, socially, or both. Traditionally cultural studies were undertaken by pitting any two groups against each other in an attempt to identify, produce, and explain differences between the two groups. It has been stressed already that a fundamental feature of culture is that it is confirmed by others and must be observed by others from the outside. This of course can be explained because individuals traditionally understand culture from the basis of their own self-identification, even if this remains in part at an unconscious level. But in reality culture is not delineated by polarized groupings such as individuals of Spanish versus Italian nationality, or, Democrat versus Republican voters in the United States.

It is now accepted that understanding culture and cultural embeddedness requires more pluralistic, multi-group approaches. This is particularly true in the modern environment where national cultures are increasingly enriched and characterized by globalization trends and greater movement of people. For example, the imprint of the late British architect Zaha Hadid on the world of architecture reflects her Middle Eastern and British background, her training in London and her commitment to modernism, among other cultural influences. It cannot be suggested with confidence that Hadid's work is an example of British architecture. Similarly, while largely composed of a population of European descent, the U.S. culture has also been shaped by the cultures of Native Americans, Latin Americans, Africans and Asians to provide a melting pot that artists reflect on and traverse. So while there may be a tendency to identify or test cultural differences in a quantifiable way, adopting tools such as Geert Hofstede's five dimensions of national culture (Hofstede 2001) or perhaps comparing Islamic and Christian banking practices, these approaches generate little insight into the embedded mechanisms underlying cultural effects.

Understanding cultural embeddedness requires a more holistic explanation involving many factors such as ethnic identity, transitory beliefs that may determine a person's communal identities and loyalties at a point in time (e.g., being "Irish" on St. Patrick's Day) (Stayman and Deshpande 1989), racial stereotyping of others, inter-generational influences, religion or language. Essentially, the components of how individuals can quantify cultural embeddedness involve an interplay of continuous dynamic interactions with each other. This speaks to a complicated fusion of mechanisms responsible for the visible cultural effects that embeds artists within a group. When outside, observers can only at best infer what these might be creating the fundamental challenge for where and how entrepreneurs can do business.

An example of the transitory and other influences on culturally embedded art is provided in Box 4.1 where the journey of "fado" music in Portugal is described. From its rise on the streets of Lisbon in the early 19th century the illustration shows how it emerged into the internationally recognized art form of today. This journey illustrates how art takes on

Box 4.1 The cultural journey of fado

Fado is a musical genre that can be traced back to the early 19th century in Lisbon although its origins are probably from a much earlier period. Some historians suggest an ancient Moorish influence. Fado is characterized by mournful tunes and lyrics, often about the sea or the life of the poor, and infused with a sense of longing. This longing is captured by the Portuguese word *Saudade* which claims no direct translation into English but purports to be characteristic of the Portuguese temperament. From its origins of spontaneous execution in gardens, bullfights, streets and alleyways, fado moved into the more theatrical representations of a bohemian aristocrat with the fado singing prostitute in the early part of the 20th century. A military coup in 1926 and subsequent censorship regulation in 1927 would however see the extinction of this type of public theater. With the consequential Estado Novo authoritarian regime Fado suffered unavoidable changes. Its emergence in fado houses in Lisbon's historic neighborhoods from the middle of the 20th century coincided with a loss of many of the original improvisation aspects of the art. Internationalization of fado consolidated in the 1950s across the African continent and in Brazil. In 1974 Portugal instituted a democratic regime. While fado initially became unpopular because of its prior association with the former Estato Novo, the stabilizing of democracy allowed fado to regain its own space. It is mainly since the 1980s and with globalization and renewed interest in local music cultures that fado would cement its position in the international World Music circuits with a new generation of talented interpreters and internally renowned performers.

the static and dynamic elements of people and place, transforming over time yet still rooted in its place and history.

Traversing Culturally Embedded Domains

Having portrayed the stable and dynamic features confronting creative industries as culturally embedded actors, it may appear intriguing that art can appeal beyond its cultural confines. Could some art be culture-free?

Or, are there degrees of cultural embeddedness? Or, perhaps is art interpreted differently across cultures while still being appreciated? Given that art forms such an important part of culture and the concepts are usually considered in tandem, many would suggest that art cannot be culture-free because it is always open to interpretation (Hacoy 2002, Greenfield 1977). Yet in the business world financial, geographical, and cultural boundaries are being broken for the purchase and sale of art. This is epitomized in the growing trend of Asian buyers that are now gravitating toward Western art (Christies 2017).

Cross-cultural researchers have determined that for a construct to traverse cultural boundaries, at least conceptual and functional equivalent must be established in another culture (Hacoy 2002; Duijker and Frijda 1960; Berry and Dasen 1974; Poortinga and Malpass 1986). With any culture, contemporary meanings are usually multiple, complex, situational, and changing. A triangulation of the diversity of voices within the cultural group and with the creator of the art may be necessary to ascertain the range of possibility in meanings. Moreover in a postmodern multicultural world, meaning structures from minority cultures have often blended with dominant culture constructs in some sophisticated, syncretized form to make this task even more challenging. It is also interesting to note that inherent bias can exist in which indigenous perspectives or non-Western perspectives are often omitted or simplistically or stereotypically represented (Said 1978; Hacoy 2002). So while interpretation is relevant within dominant culture individuals, it is exponentially more complicated with individuals from different cultural backgrounds.

Traversing cultures and overcoming bias involves sensitivity to both the interpretation of the artist and the targeted group. Local meaning structures can be discerned through consultations with community or cultural group members or through a client. Culture experts or intermediaries are well recognized in the literature ranging from community participants (Hacoy 2002) to professionals (Boutinot et al. 2015) to intermediaries (Ryan, Keane, and Cunningham 2008) that often fulfill this task.

Can Art Be Culture Free?

Could it be possible to avoid the complexity of culturally embedded enterprise or traversing art to customers across cultural groups? Although many suggest that this is not possible, there are arguments for an alternate view. While it may be somewhat aspirational to achieve in its entirety multiple logics exist for how culture-free art can exist at polarized ends of a continuum.

One notion of what it means to be culture-free may be reflected in universal *processes* of enterprise. It has been argued that the logic of industrialism generates imperatives of an economic and technical nature that molds the development of industrial societies into a common pattern (Kerr et al. 1960). Industrialization in this argument brings about certain changes in the context of organizations which necessitates certain developments in the organizational structure that are universal like shared services and systems (Hickson et al. 1974). While artistic firms are often small enterprises where universal complexities of scale may be irrelevant, these ideas can manifest in peculiar forms. Artistic professional services such as architecture are one example where professional norms, behaviors and etiquette can traverse cultural boundaries allowing organizations to establish across cultures in the same way that structural complexities of size create universal processes in large organizations. Another manifestation of culture free processes may be conceptualized in a strong artistic identity that is needed to handle the high risk and failure inherent in the sector (Bridgstock 2011; Hall 2004; Inkson 2006). This can be regarded as universal and artists may even locate to creative cities such as London, New York, Los Angeles to create exhibition opportunities but also to realize a universal expectation of identity (Lingo and Tepper 2015).

Another aspiration of culture free relates to *product*. The avant-garde theater artist Antonin Artaud was renowned for his passion-driven action in opposition to a culture. Artaud counsels us to learn from the great painters and their pictures that he suggests are able to evoke a metaphysical pathos with great themes as "Becoming," "Destiny," "Equilibrium," or "Chaos." Artaud rebelling against all forms of culture espouses that only art by those who had journeyed deeply into their own mindscapes could culture. The business of avant-garde strives for critical creativity subverting a conventional and formalized culture (Guillet de Monthoux 2005). Whether culture free product can complement entrepreneurship however is open to consideration with one proponent, the provocative Polish writer Witold Gombrowicz (1904–1969, p. 268) informing us that:

A creator cannot count on steady earnings. There is a kind of art for which you are paid and another you have to pay for performing. You may pay with your health or with your belongings. My life has been more of an ascetic kind.

Artaud has been described as both a madman and a visionary but his dialogue opens up a debate that art could *escape* from the confines of culture.

One final observation and perhaps more commercially focused than Artaud's vision of culture free art is the emergence of new forms of global iconic art such as architecture (Sklair 2005, 2006) that is driven by capitalist globalization. In earlier periods most iconic art was driven by the interests of the state and/or religion. Global art (e.g., the Disney concert hall in Los Angeles designed by the architect Frank Gehry) sponsored by institutions and agents of the transnational capitalist class has increasingly come to define the times, places and audiences that make art iconic.

Managing the Challenge of Cultural Embeddedness in the Arts

For entrepreneurs in the arts, dealing with the culturally embedded nature of their work presents particular challenges for reaching customers and other audiences. It is therefore important to understand the interplay between art and culture to gain greater insight on commercialization and growth opportunities. Suggestions for entrepreneurial artists can be synthesized into five options grounded in our evaluation of cultural embeddedness, traversing cultures, and culture-free art forms:

1. Stay local/familiar. Artistic interpretation is often culturally embedded and this chapter points to the intricacy and complexity of understanding cultural groupings. Given that culture embeds elusive and transient elements, by staying with the artist's cultural group keeps them in tune with the evolving nature of shared beliefs, values, and norms of everyday activity.
2. Use experts to interpret. Certain actors can act as cultural interpreters and intermediaries for the artist possibly naturally because they span multiple groupings but also because they may have an interest in

communicating with the artist and the community. These may include agents, government representatives, exhibition or craft fair organizers. Evidently resources will be required for this and some risk is involved in letting go of the meaning from the artist's work. However, access and connections as well as time saving may outweigh these concerns.

3. Adjust and adapt. The artist can act as an astute ethnographer in determining current and local meaning systems rather than relying on others. This requires skill and time but doing it independently means that the artist maintains control lowering potential for reputation damage. Relationships can be formed that may be enduring helping the artist to grow their business.

4. Awareness of culture-free process and product dimensions. Even if culture free art is an aspirational notion, an awareness of how either processes or product can be culture free provides a basis for decision making about business models, growth and positioning of the business.

5. Maneuver within subgroups. Rather than spanning cultural domains a focus on moving within cultural subgroups can have benefits. Minority to minority cultural groups may have a certain shared understanding. Certainly minority to majority groups may have an understanding although taking an easy option by focusing on a majority group may limit responses and persuasion.

References

Berry, J., and P. Dasen. 1974. *Introduction to Culture and Cognition*. London: Methuen.

Boutinot, A., S. Ansari, M. Belkhouja, and V. Mangematin. 2015. "Reputational Spillovers: Evidence from French Architecture." *Strategic Organization* 13, no. 4, pp. 284–306.

Bridgstock, R. 2011. "Skills for Creative Industries Graduate Success." *Education and Training* 53, no. 1, pp. 9–26.

Christies. 2017. "Hong Kong Spring Sales Season Maintains Christie's Global Leadership in Asian Art." Christies, Last Modified 31 May 2017. http://christies.com/Features/Records-tumble-during-Christies-Hong-Kong-Spring-sales-season-8366-3.aspx

DCMS. 1998. *Creative Britain: New Talents for the New Economy*. London: Department of Culture, Media and Sport.

DCMS. 2011. *Creative Industries Economic Estimates: Full Statistical Release*. London: Department of Culture, Media and Sport.

Duijker, H., and N. Frijda. 1960. *National Character and National Stereotypes*. Amsterdam: Noord-Hollandse.

Florida, R. 2007. *The Flight of the Creative Class: The New Global Competition for Talent*. New York: HarperCollins.

Greenfield, P. 1977. "Culture as Process: Empirical Methods for Cultural Psychology." In *Handbook of Cross Cultural Psychology*, eds. J. Berry, Y. Poortinga and J. Pandy, 285–301. Needham Heights, MA: Allen & Bacon.

Guillet de Monthoux, P. 2005. "Momo Management: A Note on the Insultant Antonin Artaud and his Clients." *Culture and Organization* 11, no. 4, pp. 259–68.

Hacoy, D. 2002. "Cross Cultural Issues in Art Therapy." *Art Therapy* 19, no. 4, pp. 141–45.

Hall, D. 2004. "The Protean Career: A Quarter-Century Journey." *Journal of Vocational Behaviour* 65, no. 1, pp. 1–13.

Hickson, D., C. Hinings, D. McMillan, and J. Schwitter. 1974. "The Culture Free Context of Organization Structure: A Tri-National Comparison." *Sociology* 8, no. 1, pp. 59–80.

Hofstede, G. 2001. *Culture's Consequences: Comparing Values, Behaviours, Institutions, and Organizations Across Nations*. New York: Sage Publications.

Inkson, K. 2006. "Protean and Boundaryless Careers as Methphors." *Journal of Vocational Behaviour* 69, pp. 48–63.

Kerr, C., J. Dunlop, F. Harbison, and C. Myers. 1960. *Industrialism and Industrial Man*. Cambridge, Mass: Harvard University Press.

Lingo, E., and S. Tepper. 2015. "Looking Back, Looking Forward: Arts-Based Careers and Creative Work." *Work and Occupations* 40, no. 4, pp. 337–63.

Markusen, A. 2013. "Artists Work Everywhere." *Work and Occupations* 40, no. 4, pp. 481–95.

Poortinga, Y., and R. Malpass. 1986. *Field Methods in Cross Cultural Research*, eds W. Lonner and J. Berry. Beverley Hills: Sage Publications.

Ryan, M., M. Keane, and S. Cunningham. 2008. "From Remote Outback Beginnings to Cultural Export Phenomenon: A Case Study of Finance and the Internationalization of Indigenous Australian Visual Art." In *Information Society or Knowledge Societies? UNESCO in the Smart State*, eds. R. Breit and J. Servaes, 93–110. Penang: Southbound Publications.

Said, E. 1978. *Orientalism*. New York: Random House.

Scott, A. 2006. Creative Cities: Conceptual Issues and Policy Questions. eScholarship, University of California, 17.

Shenkar, O., Y. Luo, and T. Chi. 2015. *International Business*. New York: Routledge.

Sklair, L. 2005. "The Transnational Capitalist Class and Contemporary Architecture in Globalizing Cities." *International Journal of Urban and Regional Research* 29, no. 3, pp. 485–500.

Sklair, L. 2006. "Iconic Architecture and Capitalist Globalization." *City* 10, no. 1, pp. 22–47.

Stayman, D., and R. Deshpande. 1989. "Situational Ethnicity and Consumer Behavior." *Journal of Consumer Research* 16, no. 3, pp. 361–71.

UNCTAD. 2010. Creative Economy Report. United Nations. http://unctadxiii. org/en/SessionDocument/ditctab20103_en.pdf

Whitely, W., and G. England. 1977. "Managerial Values as a Reflection of Culture and the Process of Industrialization." *Academy of Management Journal* 20, no. 3, pp. 439–53.

CHAPTER 5

Art Entrepreneurship and Internationalization at Home: Internationalization Strategies of Theaters from a Central European Country

Paraskevi Karageorgu and Andreja Jaklic

Introduction

Internationalization of art institutions has been driven by various factors. The advanced technology and shift toward its common use, which allows people from all income classes to travel (low cost airlines, bus lines, train discounts, etc.), the mass digitization and transportability not only of goods and services, but content as well and the Internet, which links people no matter their background, facilitated communication, especially due to the widespread learning of English language. These factors were enabled by trade liberalization, which is more intense especially on a regional level (e.g., the European Single Market). This unprecedented growth of intercultural contacts brought by globalization now allows citizens to "physically, legally, culturally, and psychologically engage with each other in 'one world'" (Scholte 2002, p. 14).

The chapter explores first-time internationalization strategy of small- and medium-sized enterprises (SMEs) from culture and creative industries (CCI) and discusses the opportunities of using non-nationals in the home country as a starting point for internationalization. This group of potential audiences (that has been ignored in the past), is presented as a new market segment that needs to be explored and tackled within marketing strategy, as it is becoming an increasingly relevant in terms of Single European Market (SEM). Enterprises can save resources and explore their existing international competitive advantages already at the home market. Such internationalization at home (IaH) strategy can be a helpful option for SMEs from transition and emerging markets. The chapter explores two case studies from Central and Eastern Europe, discusses the internationalization potential in the home market environment and analyzes whether internationalization has become an innovative entry mode and strategy for audience development for SMEs in CCI.

To analyze the proposed internationalization strategy, the authors follow the multi-method or mixed methods case study approach (Hurmerinta and Nummela 2011, p. 211) in data collection and analysis, since the topic is complex and combines concepts from different disciplines (international business, marketing, business environment, cultural policies, art management). The explorative research includes in-depth interviews, the enterprise's social networks profile research, management surveys, customer surveys, in-depth semi-structured interviews, and participant observation.

Internationalization in CCI

Recent empirical evidence confirmed the increased speed and diversification in internationalization strategies, being in entry modes, geographical spread, or product/services portfolio (Dikova et al. 2016). While some successful new internationalizers demonstrate high sophistication and complexity in several internationalization dimensions from the early beginnings, others still follow more experimental/learning by doing approach. Though dominant theoretical frameworks such as the OLI paradigm (Dunning 1993) or the resource base theory or the Uppsala model (Johanson and Vahlne 2009) help to understand internationalization process, recent developments in international entrepreneurship constantly demonstrate new ways and patterns of internationalization. Efforts to understand markets as networks are particularly useful to understand the strategies of newly internationalizing SMEs in CCI (Elg 2000;

Ellis 2000). Where the business environment is a "web of relationships, a network, rather than as a neoclassical market with many independent suppliers and customers" and the importance of the so called *insidership* in "relevant network(s) is necessary for successful internationalization and so by the same token there is a liability of outsidership" (Johanson and Vahlne 2009, p. 1).

EU membership and SEM has allowed many art entrepreneurs from CCI to become part of such networks, facilitating the accumulation of knowledge and leading to their internationalization. The motivation for internationalization ranges from market seeking to resource, efficiency, and strategic asset seeking (Dunning, 1993), but are most commonly summed up as audience and/or assets development.

The two terms: "artistic work" and "entrepreneurial processes" have often remained separate in terms of both academic research and practice (Zander and Scherdin 2011, p. 1). However, the economic crisis affected the cultural sector in Europe severely, as state funding was not able to secure the existence of many artists and art organizations (that rely primarily on public sources). Thus, the "entrepreneurial" approach even if not called by such term, has started to emerge as an alternative way of survival. Entrepreneurship is most commonly associated with the discovery and pursuit of new business opportunities through the creation of business firms (Gartner, 1988; Shane and Venkataraman, 2000 in Zander and Scherdin 2011). It is an activity of "uncertainty inherent in every action" and "in any real and living economy every actor is always an entrepreneur" (Mises 1949, pp. 253–54). However, as the "artists remain fundamentally suspicious of anything that has to do with commerce and business" (Zander and Scherdin 2011, p. 3), the *audience development*, is the preferred terminology of market seeking actors. Audience development is the core reason why CCIs turn to entrepreneurship, being a special branch of marketing and an expression preferred by cultural managers.

Next to core motivation is assets seeking and assets development. Here, the use of English language is a key asset and main tool for European SMEs, as it increased the opportunities on the market. The knowledge of English has become a comparative advantage over those who cannot speak English or have not adopted it in their communication (Neeley 2012, Van Parijs 2004).

However, the connection between the internationalization and the English language, specifically in the CCI is not without risks. Research in multilingual education can be applied to the CCIs claims that performance in English lacks the dimension of diversity and therefore does not adequately reflect the rhetoric of plurality and interculturality which accompanies proposals for internationalization (Liddicoat 2003). *Cultural exception* (when it comes to content travelling beyond borders) is therefore seen as important measure, especially in small countries. Slovenia, the country of the selected case studies, has two million inhabitants, yet the majority of the population or 59 percent speaks excellent English (European Commission 2012, p. 21). The market for Slovenian language is small and cultural industry suffers, as consumers can easily access the content they are interested in English and sectors such as the book industry are seriously threatened.[1] Though this can be a threat for some SMEs from CCI, it is also a turning point for the CCI to adjust and turn this phenomenon into an asset in order to promote the accessibility of their own content. The diversity of cultures can stay invisible if communication is not adopted. It does not mean only to create content in English, but first of all to stimulate local production which then is communicated also in English (official translations, subtitles). As the global expansion of English has led to the pluralization of its users, the audience has also become global (Crystal 2003). It can come from unexpected places and can be included in the audience development strategies. English offers the connection with bigger and established institutions and art groups (and their creation of value), which is often a matter of survival and represents essential framework for internationalization for art communities from small transition economies.

---

[1] Subtitles in native language are not needed, they can consume English-speaking content or content with English subtitles and they do not need local providers to find it. According to Eurobarometer younger people, particularly between 15 and 24 year old when compared with those aged 55+, are more likely to mention English (79 percent vs. 56 percent respectively), German (20 percent vs. 14 percent), Spanish (18 percent vs. 11 percent), and Chinese (8 percent vs. 4 percent) as most useful languages for personal development (European Commission 2012). This data show a trend for the future: the vast majority of the global population will most certainly speak English and will have access to the Internet.

The increasing number of networks and associations in the EU facilitates communication and performance, accumulation of knowledge, and entrepreneurship models development. It opens new markets and better platforms for expression. Introducing films, music, theater performances in SEM means a test of international potential and competitiveness and can enhance the demand for cultural content inside and outside the EU. While the strength of the U.S. cultural content is a production oriented toward international markets, taking advantage of the English language world domination, private investment, professional business models, and sophisticated marketing has proven a successful strategy (Crystal 2003, p. 99). The application of this approach in Europe however seems controversial, as culture is often funded with public money, treated as "national treasure" (i.e., public good) and closely connected to national identity.

Case Studies

The case studies were chosen in the Central and Eastern European region, recognized for dynamic liberalization, rapid transformation, and intensive integration into European and global business networks (Kaminski and Ng, 2005), which offers an excellent context for exploring early internationalization. Ljubljana, the capital of Slovenia, is an example of a destination, where the movement of people flourished in the past years, thanks to the four freedoms established in the EU.[2] Foreign visitors to Ljubljana amount to more than double its own population.[3]

As a whole, foreigners in Slovenia represent 4.95 percent (Statistical Office of the Republic of Slovenia 2016) of the population (excluding foreign students and expatriates or people in international assignment) and this has been identified as enough for demand driven IaH. Cultural institutions have recognized the demand for cultural production in

---

[2] Ljubljana's population is 287,218 people. In 2011 the visits amounted to 423,163 of which 404,969 were foreigners in 2016 this number was 726.082 (of which 690,585 were foreigners) (Municipality of Ljubljana 2017).

[3] It is also important to note that this number is higher in real terms, as data is not possible to be collected for travellers who stay with friends or use online hosting platforms.

English language, which has been primarily limited only to concerts and films from the United Kingdom and the United States (in Slovenia, films are not dubbed). The case studies presented here show two small art organizations that have recognized this potential and have shared their experience in implementing the IaH model for audience development.

The authors analyze two alternative theaters observed from July 2016 to March 2017 and their early internationalization efforts to use English, as part of their audience development strategy.[4] They are both supported by public funds, but recognized the opportunity and the need to internationalize at the same time in spite of different age, experience, and approaches in their work. In both cases, international networks have been of crucial importance for their entrance in foreign markets.

Case Study 1: IGLU—Improvisational Theatre of Ljubljana

IGLU is a crew of three performers with a professional approach to the improvisational arts. Inspired by the international movement OHANA, where the three are members, IGLU's interest in international exchange and the wish to establish a improv culture in Ljubljana led to the establishment of the theater. The first show in English was in 2011, where the potential of Ljubljana as an international hub was recognized. On the first show in English there was only one foreigner, however the domestic audience accepted the experiment well, which helped the recognize the need for more comprehensive strategy. To exploit this potential they included foreign guests, which was also provoked due to the need for know-how exchange. Knowledge transfer speeded up learning, alongside skills and network development. In a conversation with one of IGLU's founders, it was noted that he views this strategy as a "very amateur internationalisation to do every month," and finds the exchange or artists a very cost-efficient and innovative foreign market entry mode.

---

[4] The variables observed during from July 2016 to March 2017 were: number of international visitors for the performances; amount of financial public support; social network efficiency and responsiveness; management style and time dedicated to marketing strategies.

Nowadays, IGLU targets local and international audience with shows in Slovenian and in English. After five years, the number of foreign visitors are steadily growing and non-nationals in the audience have increased. On their English show in January 2017, almost half of the people were foreigners (each show has 60 to 100 visitors). In total, IGLU has three to four shows per month of which one is English, usually with a guest from abroad. About a third of the audience of the English shows are foreigners.

IaH not only helped them change the structure of audience, but also changed the need for public funds[5] and pricing policy. The main reason for internationalization was not lack of finance, but primarily from content and staff development. From conversations with IGLU, the authors found out that they see this as a long-term investment:

> without an enormous input we receive an immense output: we grow and develop our skills and way of working. There is no improv school in Slovenia, so if we want to be good in what we do and be professional, we have to go abroad.

This strategy helped them to explore the market and increase demand. Improved content, the improv school and rising demand also helped them set new pricing policy. Free tickets (that were used at the beginning, also due to availability of public funds) were substituted with market prices, followed by the increased prices for their improv school. Social networks have proven to be their best tool for advertising, with paid ads and double language posts for events. Their website is in English and Slovenian. They have also recognized the country's main event website as very good promotional tool. For them, mail list has proven to be very effective, and activated the most important marketing form: the word of mouth. The social media also stimulated marketing research and survey that helped them introduce changes (e.g., identifying the leaflets are ineffective way of advertisement).

---

[5] IGLU has stopped applying for public funds, as they have calculated the inefficiency of spending a significant amount of time of submitting documentation for small amount of public support, but rather dedicate an additional time to marketing and audience development, strategy, which has brought positive results.

The introduction to English language shows has proved as important decision for the IGLU development; foreign audience became significant part of the audience, however not at the expense of the domestic one. High level of English language knowledge in home country however influences this success. In addition, IGLU also recognized the potential of improv theater to extract the best from physical experiences and transcended language barriers.[6]

IaH strategy with foreign guests also increased their resources and capacities for direct export of their performances. With the help of Ohana—European Improv Project and ITI—International Theatresports Institute, IGLU Theatre has built a close connection with theaters in Germany, Switzerland, Canada and they have also performed in the Netherlands, Germany, Switzerland, Croatia, France, Italy, Belgium, Czech Republic, Austria, Poland, and different cities in Canada and the United States. This "internationalization" was self-financed and provoked by the need to learn, leading to their professional improv skills, defined in theory as strategic asset seeking (Dunning 1993).

Case Study 2: Glej Theatre

The Glej Theatre (founded in 1970) is one of Slovenia's oldest independent theaters. As an experimental venue and production house, renowned for unconventional theater performances it constantly undertakes new artistic approaches. Glej emerged as a response to the need for an alternative space for independent theatrical productions in Ljubljana[7] and was founded by a group of directors, inspired by the evolving experimental theater approaches abroad.

---

[6] An example being a show where there are six people on the stage who perform in their native language, which turned out to be a great successful experiment. The format of such performance is called Babylon: everyone speaks their own language and the second step of the performance consists of everyone speaking a language, which they know badly. The key here is to act with your body.

[7] The theater and its experimental nature were highly influenced by the Polish innovative theater director Jerzy Grotowski the American Professor of Performance Studies Richard Schechner (Arhar 2010).

Business models and financing alternatives for Glej have proven very unstable. The most important source is public funding; however this has been declining constantly in the last decade. At the same time new opportunities opened up with Slovenia's accession to the EU.

Glej collaborates with numerous local theaters, but in terms of innovation, it is pioneering the introduction of English language performances. Every first Saturday of the month "Glej in English" is held, a program established in 2013. This special program is presented as "performances that are performed in English or have English subtitles, aimed at foreign citizens living in Slovenia," as stated on Glej's official website. Going "international" therefore meant the translation of original Glej's content and it had three purposes: (1) to enlarge the theater's audience, including the international community in Ljubljana, (2) to allow the theater to travel and present their shows abroad (exports), and (3) to become an international theater hub for professionals (assets seeking and innovation cooperation).

Thus, they expose Slovenian productions to non-nationals and guest productions to locals. By this exchange, the process of Glej travelling abroad (exports of production) has also been facilitated. Foreign audience represents between 20 and 40 percent of Glej performances (Čater 2016). Another very important target audience for Glej are theater professionals, as it has become a meeting point for foreign theater professionals, who recognize Glej as an innovative regional experimental theater hub. Glej is using several options; they present a show in English when they are guest performances or have it both ways when they present a Slovenian show with English subtitles. Such inclusive performances diversify and develop the audience and improve the access to the Slovenian cultural scene for foreigners.

Internationalization outside home market is (still) regionally concentrated. Most of Glej's travels is in the culturally, linguistically and geographically close countries of ex-Yugoslavia, which is aiding the success of such collaborations. Extensions beyond the region are facilitated by the International Network for Contemporary Performing Arts (IETM). Glej is part of the network and for the past five years they performed in Spain, Netherlands, France, Tunisia, Litva, Austria, Hungary, and the United States. International network helped them to recognize new market segments and opportunities for both: audience and assets development. The importance of EU for Glej is significant as EU funds are perceived as a great way for the internationalization of small European theaters and almost the only way. In this light, they see the success rate of EU funds absorption for the cultural sector in Slovenia as very low.[8]

The theater uses different channels (e.g., Embassies, Erasmus networks, professional associations, etc.) and relies on social networks communication. It is also listed in Ljubljana's tourist web page, which is available in nine languages.

Conclusions

The examined case studies showed IaH as useful strategy for audience development, access to resources development, creation of value and market extension. However, the success of this strategy is vitally related to the presence of international network; membership in an international organization allows access to resources, channels to communicate own content, fast implementation of "best practices" and innovation cooperation, which are all important for small countries. Both theaters have improved the access to original Slovenian theater productions for foreigners by the use of English language.

The proposition that art institutions should go international in order to enlarge and stabilize domestic production has been demonstrated in the presented case studies. Audience and assets development are essential for the survival of art organizations, in financial terms, but also in terms of following new trends and being part of the global art movements. Summing up, internationalization at home does not endanger the national art and culture, but may on the contrary bring synergies if IaH

---

[8] One of the most influential international projects for Glej is Generation to Generation (G2G), cofunded by the European Union. Different theaters have realized that there is a trend of decline of young audiences in most European countries. Slovenia is no exception, as young people between 12 and 19 do not have content to be shown, while children and adults have many programs to choose from. G2G therefore became an European project, coordinated by Glej trying to deal with this challenge together with partners from 11 EU countries.

strategy is designed systematically. The studied cases demonstrated that the speed and scope of internationalization without IaH would have been substantially lower.

In one way or another, internationalization at home, with globalized product (performances in English), is a trend present all over Europe, as cities are becoming more and more multicultural. The accessibility of cultural activities is crucial for integration, so the adoption of such internationalization models may support the integration process and become effective strategy of art and cultural institutions to (re)position themselves in the European and global art scene.

References

Arhar, N. November, 2010. "40 let gledališča Glej." *RTV Slovenija.*

Čater, T. January, 2016. "Predstava z nadnapisi ne izgubi nič bistvenega, pridobi pa tuje občinstvo." *MMC RTV Slovenija.*

Crystal, D. 2003. *English as a Global Language.* 2nd ed. Cambridge: Cambridge University Press.

Dikova, D., A. Jaklič, A. Burger, and A. Kunčič. February, 2016. "What Is Beneficial for First-Time SME-Exporters from a Transition Economy: A Diversified or a Focused Export-strategy?" *Journal of World Business* 51, no. 2, pp. 185–99.

Elg, U. March, 2000. "Firms' Home–Market Relationships: Their Role when Selecting International Alliance Partners." *Journal of International Business Studies* 31, no. 1, pp. 169–77.

Ellis, P.D. January, 2000. "Social Ties and Foreign Market Entry." *Journal of International Business Studies* 31, no. 33, pp. 443–69.

European Commission. 2012. Europeans and Their Languages Report. Special Barometer 386. http://ec.europa.eu/commfrontoffice/publicopinion/archives/ebs/ebs_386_en.pdf

Hurmerinta, L., and N. Nummela. 2011. "Mixed Method Case studies in International Business Research." In *Rethinking the Case Study in International Business and Management Research.* Cheltenham: Edward Elgar Publishing.

Johanson, J., and J.E. Vahlne. December, 2009. "The Uppsala Internationalization Process Model Revisited: From Liability of Foreignness to Liability of Outsidership." *Journal of International Business Studies* 40, pp. 1411–31.

Kaminski, B., and F. Ng. January, 2005. "Production Disintegration and Integration of Central Europe into Global markets." *International Review of Economics & Finance* 14, pp. 377–90.

Liddicoat, A. 2003. "Internationalisation as a Concept in Higher Education: Perspectives from Policy." In *Australian Perspectives on Internationalising Education*. Melbourne: Language Australia.

Municipality of Ljubljana 2017. Statistični podatki v letih 2002–2016. *https:// visitljubljana.com/sl/medijsko-sredisce-b2b/statistika/statisticni-podatki-v-letih-2002-2016/*

Neeley, T. May, 2012. "Global Business Speaks English." *Harvard Business Review*.

Scholte, J. 2002. "What is Globalisation? The Definitional issue—Again." *Centre for the Study of Globalisation and Regionalisation*. Coventry: University of Warwick. Working Paper 109/02, pp. 1–34.

Statistical Office of the Republic of Slovenia. May, 2016. *Izdana dovoljenja za prebivanje*. http://stat.si/statweb

Van Parijs, P. April, 2004. "Europe's Linguistic Challenge." *European Journal of Sociology* 45, no. 1, pp. 113–54.

Zander, I., and M. Scherdin. 2011. "Art Entrepreneurship: An Introduction." *Art Entrepreneurship*. Cheltenham: Edward Elgar Publishing.

PART III

Pathways to Growth and Success

CHAPTER 6

Exploring the Emergence of Contemporary Art Galleries in Istanbul: The Effectuation Perspective

Aytug Sozuer

The annual sales volume in global art market from 2007 to 2016 was around $60 billion on average (McAndrew 2017). With respect to Turkey's 0.9 percent share in world trade, the country's art market can be roughly estimated to be around $500 million. In terms of contemporary art, which refers to works by artists born after 1945, the global auction revenues reached above $1 billion in recent years (Artprice 2014). Given that there are 1.6 times more sales in dealers than in auctions (Pownall 2017), the world contemporary art market can be estimated over $2.5 billion. In 2011, the auction revenue from contemporary art in Turkey reached $7.5 million (Artprice 2012). Although this figure seemed relatively low in percentage, Turkey became one of the top ten global marketplaces for contemporary art in that year, which encouraged many to set foot on the supply side. In the following five years, the number of galleries increased over 50 percent, which also created a rush among early career artists. However, the questions remained open whether the challenges of finding new clients or manageability of operational costs were properly addressed by these ventures. This study explores the dynamics behind the proliferation of contemporary art galleries in this context.

At first glance, the growth rate of contemporary art sales looks highly appealing. The auction turnover in this segment rose by 1,800 percent in 15 years. On the other hand, the market is very concentrated. Almost

85 percent of sales is realized only in three countries, namely United States, China, and the UK. The highest selling 100 contemporary artists generate around 70 percent of world auction revenue among 49,000 listed artists in the auctions (Artprice 2015). Furthermore, considering 300,000 businesses involved in art dealing around the world, 5,000 of them account up to 80 percent of total sales by value (McAndrew 2017). This inclination in the market poses a threat for smaller dealers.

Two core functions of an art gallery are (a) building trust through specialist knowledge and credibility in the market and (b) taking the risk by launching artists in early-stage and share their successes as they grow in the long run. However, when the market becomes centered, more established galleries can pick the seasoned artists from smaller galleries, which have actually borne the cost of developing an artist. If smaller galleries cannot collect decent returns, the market does not function properly. Moreover, increasing costs such as rents, exhibiting at international fairs, and other commercial expenses would escalate pressure on many galleries. Further, young artists generally lack enough financial resources to support their productions or even their living, which makes it more difficult for galleries to discover talent. In the same manner, a recent survey reports the top four business concerns of art dealers as; finding new clients, sourcing new works, costs of attending art fairs, and making acceptable profits at the year-end (Pownall 2017). Another study highlights 30 percent of all art galleries run at a loss (Resch 2016a). With regard to these macro conditions in the world art market, the following section will briefly explain the peculiarities of the Turkish setting.

Brief Chronology of Contemporary Art in Turkey

Painting in the form of modern art in Turkey can be traced back to the middle of 19th century. Starting from 1839, *Tanzimat* (meaning reorganization) reforms in the Ottoman Empire pursued the transformation of the traditional state system to a modern one. As a matter of fact, the new provisions were under the influence of European ideas. The state used art as one of the anchors for this Westernization project and a small elite sponsored artists and their productions for a long time. The state-led modernization of Turkey took a different scheme after the foundation of the Republic in 1923. However, art was still under the patronage of the state. During the 1950s and 1960s, there were only singular examples of avant-garde who traveled Europe (particularly France) and created conceptual art. With respect to movements around the world in the 1970s, critical stance arose and further artistic investigations in visual form emerged. In the 1980s, Turkey started a transition to a freer market and the growing capital generated a new elite. Through the fundamental changes in the country, the art scene became more significant. To name a few developments in this decade, serial collective exhibitions were organized, innovative techniques such as photography and video were applied to the artistic inquiry, banks and several rich people improved their art collections, and Istanbul Biennial was established. In the 1990s, drastic shifts in world political map encouraged multicultural encounters in many aspects. Turkey was one of the non-Western contexts to be discovered, especially in terms of art voice. This period was marked by growing international exchange of contemporary art and the emergence of curators in the country (Demir 2013; Madra 2015).

Since the beginning of the 2000s, Turkey has been undergoing another reconstruction era in which political and sociocultural tendencies have become crystallized. Stability, security, and economic progress have been the major concerns of the society. Indeed, income per capita increased almost threefold in 10 years and a class of newly affluent was consequently born. Among others, the market started seeking high culture as well, while *Istanbul Biennial, Istanbul Modern*; the first private contemporary art museum in Turkey, and *Contemporary Istanbul*; an internationally renowned art fair were attached to the city's identity, being the country's capital of culture (Kahraman 2014). The number of Istanbul Biennial visitors increased more than tenfold in 10 years with 545,000 in 2015 compared to 51,000 in 2005. Istanbul Modern Museum is visited by an average of 1,500 visitors every day. The trend of attraction for Contemporary Istanbul fair was also increased since its inception in 2006 (Table 6.1). Furthermore, the growing number of art faculties, creations of young artists, the establishment of new museums and supporting institutions, the proliferation of galleries, intense activities of auction houses, and relatively fast buying/collecting decisions were the prominent features of the art scene. The market witnessed historically

Table 6.1 Contemporary Istanbul statistics in brief

	2006	2007	2008	2009	2010	2011	2012	2013	2014	2015
Number of galleries	49	73	56	73	80	90	102	95	108	102
Number of artists	150	379	238	307	420	526	612	748	520	790
Number of visitors (1,000)	37.5	42	48	52	53	62	68	72	77	84
Sold/exhibited works (%)	74	61	56	68	83	75	66	67	72	64

Sources: Istanbul Art News, 2014 and Contemporary Istanbul, 2015.

high sales volumes in this period. For example, the average annual auctions sales in seasons from 2011 to 2013 were over $8 million (Artprice 2011; 2012; 2013; 2014).

Nevertheless, the recent contraction status suggests that it could be due to a speculative wave in the market and many productions and prices were actually inflated, particularly from 2009 to 2012. At the time being, there seems to be a consensus among stakeholders that the 2010s is the adjustment term for the contemporary art market in Turkey, especially in the sense of artist-gallery-collector relationships.

Art Galleries in Istanbul

It is known that the first privately owned art gallery in Istanbul was established in 1947 (Baraz 2013). The art scene was in its infancy and there were very few attempts in art dealing during the following two decades. The 1970s and 80s were more fruitful due to strengthened artistic works and accumulated wealth after liberalization policies. A handful of respected galleries were opened in this period. Especially banks and newly rich class started building up their art collections through galleries and auction houses (Kahraman 2014). In the 1990s, the market for modern art saturated and new interest rose in contemporary art, which naturally led to more variety. The contemporary art scene gained momentum in the 2000s in respect to increasing numbers of young artists, curators, galleries, institutions, publications, collectors, and art lovers in general.

As of May 2017, there were at least 45 for-profit contemporary art galleries in Istanbul. Over 85 percent of them were located within the 2-km radius of *Taksim Square*. Notably, the figure of newer galleries is significant as shown in Table 6.2.[1]

At the time being, contemporary art galleries in Istanbul face several difficulties: (1) The business turns into a profession characterized by art fairs and auctions. Specialty knowledge is being replaced with financial and social capital; (2) participating in international art fairs are costly and incentives from the public budget for this effort are very limited;

---

[1] The list is compiled from various sources and does not include galleries belonging to institutions such as museums and foundations.

Table 6.2 Number of contemporary art galleries in Istanbul

Period founded	Galleries	Share (%)
2001 and earlier	11	24
2002–06	4	9
2007–11	14	31
2012–16	16	36
Total	45	100

(3) 18 percent VAT rate on sold items is perceived high, considering the cultural aspect of the business; (4) the number of avid collectors is low. There are buyers who act as investors, asking high discounts from galleries; (5) many collectors lost confidence in the market due to earlier opportunistic pricing policy and now follow the trend of buying works from more established galleries abroad; (6) too many organized auctions have the possibility to harm the exchanges through galleries; (7) there are too few critics who would expertly appraise the value of art works; (8) rents are increasing due to gentrification in the city. Depending on the location, size, exhibitions, and number of staff, the operational costs of a modest gallery varies between $10,000 and $30,000 per month; (9) the competition between galleries gets more intense as online sale platforms are launched and works of foreign famous artists are imported to the market; and (10) galleries are being physically upgraded, which require substantial financial resources. Small white cube business model is not likely to survive in the middle run. Between 2014 and 2016, at least eight galleries were closed down.

Despite these challenges, it is evident that new galleries keep opening up in Istanbul and the underlying factors are worth examining. The following section will elaborate this phenomenon on the effectuation logic.

Effectual Reasoning and the Establishment of More Art Galleries

Sarasvathy's (2001; 2008) effectuation theory distinguishes two types of new venture creation processes as causation and effectuation. She contrasts these distinct logics in terms of choice sets and describes it this way:

"…choosing between means to create a particular effect, versus choosing between many possible effects using a particular set of means" (Sarasvathy 2001, p. 245). One of her simplified examples on the processes is requiring an artist to paint a particular person's portrait (causation) in contrast to giving the artist a blank canvas together with some paints and let the artist paint whatever he or she decides (effectuation). In the context of entrepreneurship, although the ultimate aim is to be successful, the flow between means and ends is different in this dichotomy. However, the theory proposes that, for a given set of action, it is neither practical nor possible to use algorithms and calculate expected returns when environmental uncertainty prevails. Therefore, instead of analyzing alternatives to make the rational choice as causal models suggest, the entrepreneur takes a step based on the affordability of the trial while strengthening the connections within the network to hedge the experiment (Chandler et al. 2011). Noticeably, use of this theory is encouraged in the relevant literature (e.g., Perry, Chandler, and Markova 2012; Read and Sarasvathy 2005; Read, Song, and Smit 2009).

Effectual reasoning consists of five heuristic principles (SfEA 2017):

- Bird-in-hand (starting with the available means): Before creating a new venture, entrepreneurs look into who they are, what they know, and whom they know at first, then build up possibilities on these means.
- Affordable loss (focusing on the downside risk): Entrepreneurs limit risk by contemplating how much they can afford in case of failure throughout the steps of the undertaking.
- Lemonade (leveraging contingencies): Entrepreneurs recognize all critical incidents as opportunities that can be exploited, instead of trying to avoid unexpected changes.
- Patchwork quilt (forming partnerships): In early stages of the venture, entrepreneurs pursue forming alliances and obtain pre-commitments from key stakeholders to reduce uncertainty.
- Pilot-in-the-plane (control vs. predict the future): Entrepreneurs do not assume that the future is uncontrollable; rather they are aware that their actions can actually shape it.

After this brief description of the effectual logic, its principles will be associated with the increase of contemporary art galleries in the next part.

The Research and Findings

Istanbul Art News is a content-rich art magazine and has published 11 issues a year since August 2013. It is in B3 paper size (13.9 × 19.7 in.) having 90 to 100 pages in each issue and includes supplements for the art market, literature, and architecture. All 43 issues until May 2017 are reviewed for this study and relevant scripts from news and articles on galleries and interviews with the owners, especially the newcomers, are retrieved for content analysis. The following inferences are based on this secondary data.

- *Starting with the available means principle*: These entrepreneurs were already art lovers. They have always followed art and developed a taste. Many of them were educated in an area related to art. Some of them wanted to become an artist and some of them were collectors themselves. There were also many of them who used to work for a gallery and later opened their own at some point. Thus, entrepreneurs were obviously aware that they wanted to be in this scene and somehow building up connections in the community. Furthermore, the timing for the venture was generally related to the moment they found the right location/space.
- *Focusing on the downside risk principle*: It is well-known fact that attending art fairs abroad is costly because it requires consistency and operational sense, it takes lots of time and effort. However, galleries have to be in the international arena to introduce their artists and grow their client base. Instead of making this significant investment with a dubious rate of return, many of them prefer organizing common exhibits/projects with foreign galleries. Several galleries acknowledge this way as less costly and more to the point. Another economical endeavor is to open a project space. Generally, galleries organize one exhibit per month. However, there might

be more young artists or collections deserving to be displayed. What several galleries do is to rent a smaller place in alternative locations and give rookies a chance. In this way, the main showroom would not be occupied for more risky projects.

- *Leveraging contingencies principle*: Many galleries went out of business in recent years after the speculative wave in the market ended and purchases contracted. However, the entrepreneurs who understand the gallery business is not a short-term prospect and requires maintenance of enduring relationships with artists and collectors in order to make modest amount of money in the middle run persisted and opened their galleries. Meanwhile, a new type of competition arose: online art shops. Since these platforms do not have physical places, they save huge costs and are able to set lower markups on items. Nevertheless, avid galleries reacted to this by launching their own online shops.

- *Forming partnerships principle*: Creating alliances is a typical inter-organizational activity in many business fields. One of the particular examples for galleries is to collaborate with international museums. Once a represented art takes part in established museum collections, it turns into a significant reference for the gallery. Another noteworthy initiation is the Contemporary Art Galleries Solidarity in Istanbul. These mostly young 15 galleries have come together to act jointly against speculators in the art market, to gain bargaining power in response to increasing art fair attendance fees, and so on.

- *Control versus predict the future principle*: One of the biggest obstacles in the Istanbul market is the small number of noble collectors. Thus, galleries target young people, aged between 25 and 40, and encourage them to spend even a little money on art, hoping to convert them into collectors of the future. Galleries also offer limited edition art, which appeals to art lovers with lower budgets, aiming to expand the total market. Several galleries go into publishing to establish eminence and enjoy some media power. In addition, there are some entrepreneurs, who opened branches in London or Berlin to *export* local art and show presence in world's focal spots of contemporary art.

All these features are assumed to illustrate that effectuation is an applicable lens to explain the proliferation of contemporary art galleries in Istanbul.

Conclusion

Contemporary art in Turkey has begun developing in the 1970s and 80s. In the 1990s, general public interest in contemporary art has increased, and was accompanied with international exposure. The 2000s was the period when institutions have spread and the market has started to deepen. Although a downward trend in sales volumes is acknowledged in recent years; the number of contemporary art galleries has kept rising significantly in Istanbul. The purpose of this study was to clarify the underlying factors relating to this observation. Based on anecdotal evidence, it is interpreted that entrepreneurs are most likely using *effectual reasoning* to create their ventures (contemporary art galleries) even under presumably adverse circumstances.

In constantly transforming exchange structures and processes, art galleries would hardly survive in their conventional business model. After an extensive research, Resch (2016b) makes several suggestions in terms of art gallery management. As a matter of fact, many galleries begin with small steps in the undertaking due to capital constraints. However, it is pointed out that, it is not quite sustainable. Galleries should adopt state-of-the-art business making rules. First of all, functions such as marketing, public relations, legal, and general management should be professionalized. Alliances should be formed heavily with institutions rather than with competitors. Additional features should be launched as in online platforms or publishing. Extra moneymaking options should be integrated, for example, thematic gift shops or patisseries (Resch 2016b). Finally, it truly requires aspiration, persistence, and doing things right to become a successful contemporary art gallery.

References

Artprice. 2011. *Contemporary Art Market 2010/2011*. https://artprice.com/artmarketinsight/reports (accessed February 2, 2017).

Artprice. 2012. *Contemporary Art Market 2011/2012*. https://artprice.com/artmarketinsight/reports (accessed February 2, 2017).

Artprice. 2013. *Contemporary Art Market the Artprice Annual Report 2013*. https://artprice.com/artmarketinsight/reports (accessed February 2, 2017).

Artprice. 2014. *Contemporary Art Market 2014*. https://artprice.com/artmarketinsight/ reports (accessed February 2, 2017).

Artprice. 2015. *The Contemporary Art Market Report 2015*. https://artprice.com/artmarketinsight/reports (accessed February 2, 2017).

Baraz, Y. 2013. *Artists, Dealers, Collectors*. Istanbul: Galeri Baraz Publishing.

Chandler, G.N., D.R. DeTienne, A. McKelvie, and T.V. Mumford. 2011. "Causation and Effectuation Processes: A Validation Study." *Journal of Business Venturing* 26, pp. 375–90.

Contemporary Istanbul. 2015. The 10th Edition of Contemporary Istanbul Concludes With a Record Number of Visitors. http://contemporaryistanbul.com/assets/pdfDocs/ci-closing-press-release-16-11-15-24050.pdf? (accessed April 4, 2017).

Demir, D. 2013. "Istanbul." In *Art Cities of the Future: 21st CenturyAvant-Gardes*, eds. A.I. Byrd and R. Shier. London: Phaidon Press.

Istanbul Art News. 2014. "Istatistiklerle Contemporary Istanbul." 15, p. 23.

Kahraman, H.B. 2014. *Contemporary Art in Turkey*. Istanbul: Mas Print.

Madra, B. 2015. "The Various Stages and Developments of Contemporary Art in Turkey (1990-2015)." In *User's Manual 2.0: Contemporary Art in Turkey 1975–2015*, eds. H. Altındere and S. Evren. Berlin: Revolver Publishing.

McAndrew, C. 2017. *The Art Market 2017*. Switzerland: Art Basel and UBS.

Perry, J.T., G.N. Chandler, and G. Markova.2012."Entrepreneurial Effectuation: A Review and Suggestions for Future Research."*Entrepreneurship Theory and Practice* 36, pp. 837–61.

Pownall, R.A.J. 2017. *TEFAF Art Market Report 2017*. Netherlands: The European Fine Art Foundation.

Read, S., M. Song, and W. Smit. 2009. "A Meta-Analytic Review of Effectuation and Venture Performance."*Journal of Business Venturing* 24, pp. 573–87.

Read, S., and S.D. Sarasvathy. 2005. "Knowing What to Do and Doing What You Know Effectuation as a Form of Entrepreneurial Expertise." *The Journal of Private Equity* 9, no. 1, pp. 45–62.

Resch, M. 2016a. *The Global Art Gallery Report 2016*. London: Phaidon Press.

Resch, M. 2016b. *Management of Art Galleries*. London: Phaidon Press.

Sarasvathy, S.D. 2001. "Causation and Effectuation: Toward a Theoretical Shift From Economic Inevitability to Entrepreneurial Contingency." *Academy of Management Review* 26, no. 2, pp. 243–63.

Sarasvathy, S.D. 2008. *Effectuation: Elements of Entrepreneurial Expertise.* Cheltenham: Edward Elgar Publishing.

Society for Effectual Action (SfEA). 2017. *What is Effectuation.* http://effectuation. org/sites/default/files/documents/effectuation-3-pager.pdf (accessed April 1, 2017).

CHAPTER 7

ARTrepreneurship: Shifting to a Business Mindset in a Creative World

Sonia BasSheva Mañjon and Melissa Crum

Introduction

The model of a successful artist has changed. The genius forming masterpieces in solitude soon to be serendipitously discovered is not a sustainable or an easily replicable framework to begin a successful creative enterprise. However, many artists still hold onto this model as the only possible career path. Therefore, it is imperative that educators interested in supporting the entrepreneurial dreams of artists de-mystify the passion centered trajectory, stress that commodifying their craft is not creative blasphemy, explain that the art world is not grounded in meritocracy, and demonstrate how collaboration is the key to success. Educators should combine the theoretical in-class instruction with a practicum to help shape what the authors refer to as ARTrepreneurship. An ARTrepreneur is a resourceful person who merges their artistic skills and business expertise to establish a sustainable career. The artist should understand their value—how to emotionally and/or functionally offer value to their customers and associate a monetary value to their creative endeavor manifesting into a lucrative career. Under the leadership of Dr Sonia Manjon, The Barnett Center for Integrated Arts and Enterprise at The Ohio State University (OSU) in Columbus, Ohio, sought to determine how to teach business skills to art students and local artists.

Columbus, Ohio is ranked the 6th most creative city in the United States (Wallace 2016). However, the research grounding this ranking does not reflect local artistic entrepreneurs' level of success or the business support available to make a creative enterprise profitable. "Artists are self-employed at much higher rates than others in the workforce. About 34 percent of artists in the United States are self-employed, 3.5 times the national workforce average" (Clifford 2013). Columbus has several professional development programs to support this growing population: Business of Art workshops by Wild Goose Creative, Artist Production Development Workshops by The Lincoln Theater, Educators' Summer Studio by Columbus College of Art and Design (CCAD), Columbus Writers' Workshop by Columbus Creative Cooperative, as well as programs facilitated by Ohio Design Craftsmen, McConnell Arts Center, ROY G BIV Gallery, Ohio Alliance for Arts Education and VSA Ohio led workshops. However, none are long-term comprehensive programs for art-centered businesses and students who are aspiring arts entrepreneurs. Other arts-based co-working facilities such as Columbus Idea Foundry, Ethical Art Collective, and Glass Axis provide space for artists to hone their craft, but an opportunity for these artists to learn how to use their arts for sustainable careers is missing.

Historically, business incubators focused heavily on early-stage technology companies. Conversely, according to the National Business Incubation Association, the U.S. houses roughly 1,500 incubators for start-ups, and an increasing number of them focus on niches that were previously overlooked (Goodman 2015) including the art and design industries. Ann Markusen, director of the University of Minnesota Humphrey School of Public Affairs and author of the Kauffman report, argues that arts-based entrepreneurs have unique challenges, thus often times fall through the cracks in traditional workforce and small business development programs (Clifford 2013). *The ARTrepreneur Workshop Series* (AWS) prevents artists from falling through the cracks. AWS is an incubator that offers two unique components to address the needs of OSU entrepreneurial students and Columbus artists: (1) intensive series on finance, marketing, and law; and (2) continued professional development through quarterly arts-centered business programs sponsored by The Barnett Center and Creative Control Festival (CCF). These components satiate the need for business-oriented skill building, time to focus on their businesses, and support community building and collaborations. The goal of The Barnett

Center and partners is to facilitate an ongoing study of success of arts-based entrepreneurs using our collaborative ARTrepreneur curriculum.

In early 2015, The Barnett Center and Mosaic Education Network, targeted OSU students and aspiring and early career arts-based business owners to participate in a two-part two hour interactive dialogue, *ARTrepreneur Roundtable*, to discover the needs of arts-based entrepreneurs. Participants identified three necessities for entrepreneurial success: building effective networks, acquiring business skills, and identifying time and space to work. Based on these needs, the *ARTrepreneur Workshop Series* was developed as an intensive series for students as well as new and aspiring arts-based business owners. The inaugural year was an 8-week intensive funded through a grant from Greater Columbus Arts Council (GCAC), a city-funded agency, with the goal of supporting 15 ARTrepreneurs. The center more than quadrupled its goal with an initial enrollment of 75 artists. Together with Mosaic Education Network, Creative Control Fest (CCF), Wild Goose Creative, CCAD, The Small Business Development Center, accountants, and tax professionals, the center offered a comprehensive curriculum for artists to become arts-centered business owners. In 2017, the funding was a combination of university resources with city funds. Based on feedback from former participants, the center changed the time from morning to evening, changed the program from a 3-day week/eight week series to a 5-day week/4-week series, and offered college credit for students. In 2017, 114 artists registered combining OSU students and alumni with Columbus artists. It is through this program that artists are encouraged to work, live, and play in a city dedicated to helping the creative class.

The purpose of this chapter is to offer insight to faculty establishing arts entrepreneur programs and working with art students to prepare them to lead sustainable and profitable careers after graduation. Through collaborative efforts with arts organizations and artists, The Barnett Center was able to co-create a cohort-based learning model based on the premise that creative skill and passion is not enough to be a successful ARTrepreneur. The focus of the *ARTrepreneur Workshop Series* is to show how partnerships between the academy and the community effectively shape curriculum by hiring workshop facilitators that have professional experience in both creative and business centered industries. The goal is to ensure students and arts-based business owners have the knowledge and practical skills to have sustainable careers in our changing economic times.

The Importance of Teaching Through Community/ University Partnerships

The Barnett Center for Integrated Arts and Enterprise seeks to actively engage and collaborate with artists, arts organizations, and art businesses to identify ways to effectively train students to work in the arts and to explore ways it can support the local arts communities. The mission is to educate and prepare students for successful careers in the arts and related entrepreneurial fields. The Barnett Center advances and increases students' understanding of the business side of the arts and the worlds of arts management, policy, and culture by focusing on the entrepreneurial aspects of the arts. This cannot be achieved in a vacuum, so it was necessary to combine community partners in every aspect of programming, from the speaker series to training workshops and events.

The Barnett Center wanted to ensure that the programming offered to students and the community satisfied the needs of aspiring early career artists. Therefore, The Barnett Center partnered with Dr Melissa Crum of Mosaic Education Network to lead a series of roundtables to discuss the needs of art students and the creative community. Dr Crum, facilitated the *ARTrepreneur Roundtables*—a two-part two-hour dialogue using a World Cafe framework, to discover the needs of art students, Columbus artists, and arts-based businesses. World Cafe is a method that engages large groups of people in a series of small meaningful conversations. Trained in hosting solution-based collaborative conversations and qualitative research, Dr Crum guided participants of the *ARTrepreneur Roundtables* through a World Cafe interactive process to ensure diverse contribution across artistic fields, connect perspectives on how the Barnett Center can support the arts community, extract patterns in responses, and share discoveries.

The *ARTrepreneur Roundtables* began with a collective of students, artists, and arts business owners convened in a large group discussion. This process provided the most effective approach to support local artists and OSU students affiliated with programs such as The Barnett Center's Future Arts Managers & Entrepreneurs (FAME) student organization, Fisher School of Business Entrepreneurship Association, and The Music, Media, and Enterprise Minor program located in the School of Music. Participants introduced themselves by answering the following question: "In one sentence, tell us what is your work in the world?" The introduction was meant to bring everyone's voice to the table and to hear who was in the room. After the introduction, there were three rounds of small table conversations with no more than four to five participants each. The participants simultaneously converse at their table for 20 minutes with a volunteer table host recording key issues in which the table participants determine important points. The notes are left at the table with the volunteer host for the next group. For each round, participants move to a new table, the hosts at each table shares with their new group the main points from the previous group. Each new group will then choose a new host as they deliberate the new question.

The round table questions sought to unearth the needs, current obstacles to success, and how to provide solutions. Question one: "In regards to your work in the world, what do you wish you knew earlier that you know now?" The goal was for participants to think about potential training and education needed for early artists and students entering into art centered arenas. Question two: "How would you describe the current arts community in Columbus?" It was important that the participants described their ideas contextually and not simply create a list of adjectives. Follow up questions included: What's the (creative) scene? Is it thriving? Are there industry or demographic silos? Is access to resources easy? Do people share information? What is your relationship to this art community? With the table host, each group determined two strengths in the Columbus arts community and two areas that needed support. Each group wrote the answers on Post-It notes and placed them on the wall to be categorized by Dr. Crum. The goal was to have participants consider the pros and cons of the Columbus arts community, where support is established, where it is needed, and possible areas The Barnett Center could support with added resources. Question 3: "What do you need in order to effectively execute your work in the world?" Participants were asked to state the information, resources, funding, human capital, and skills they believed are needed in order to be successful. With the table host, each group determined two to five needs associated with a business goal or project for themselves or their organization. Each group posted the answers on a separate wall and Dr. Crum categorized them. The objective was for participants to think about current and future projects, initiatives, goals as artists and arts-based organizations, and how collaborations might occur. The World Cafe interactive framework allowed The Barnett Center to create an opportunity for students and artists from various industries, artistic mediums, and demographics to interact with each other and focus on local challenges. Additionally, the framework ensured that next step solutions came directly from the participants. The process prioritized the voices of students and community artists in order to avoid an institutional top-down approach to serving the community.

The participants identified three necessities for entrepreneurial success: (1) build networks with other creatives (artists, designers, writers, and performers), (2) acquire business skills, and (3) have time and working space to focus on creative projects. These outcomes were the basis for designing the *ARTrepreneur Workshop Series*. The authors invited local artists and OSU students to participate in an annual summer cohort with arts-based business owners to focus on business needs to support career and economic success. AWS supports talented students and community artists to gain practical business skills and increase self-confidence to strengthen their economic, social, and artistic vitality in a specific neighborhood on the brink of revitalization. The program was piloted in the Franklinton district due to existing relationships with organizations located there. Franklinton had a reputation as a poor crime-stricken area known as "the Bottoms." But as artists entered the area they began to redirect the city's revitalization efforts targeting Columbus' progressive and diverse creatives. Former mayor of Columbus, Michael B. Coleman stated, "I want [Franklinton] to be a place where the young, creative class of people live and develop ideas of the future in an electric and energetic environment."

AWS supported artists across the city who needed time, community, and business acumen to achieve success and sustainability. The authors' unique approach to teaching arts-based business development had three goals: (1) to deepen student engagement with art-based professionals for career success, (2) create opportunities for experienced and aspiring artists, arts-based business owners, and students by building an intellectual community with the Barnett Center and other partners, and (3) integrate local arts-based business owners that have the practical business skills and creative experiences to facilitate workshops. It was discovered that it's ineffective to have studio art professors teach ARTrepreneurs, it is equally ineffective to have traditional business professionals teach ARTrepreneurs. Instead, a hybrid of professionals entrenched in the creative industry was needed along with expertise in the business side of their artistry.

ARTrepreneur Workshop Series

AWS brings together a variety of partners committed to creating solutions for arts-based entrepreneurs using a collaborative ARTrepreneur curricular approach. The first cohort started summer 2016 as an initiative for students and creative entrepreneurs to support the development of their creative careers. This pilot program was supported by an $18,000 grant from the Greater Columbus Arts Council (GCAC) to test the authors' theory of providing a practicum by which both students and Columbus artists could co-create solutions for arts-based entrepreneurs using a collaborative ARTrepreneur curricular approach. The 8-week pilot met 3 days per week from May 3 to June 23, 2016 at the STEAM Factory in The Franklinton. Founded in December 2012 by a collection of young and energetic Ohio State faculty, postdocs and staff, the STEAM Factory is a diverse and inclusive grass-roots network in the Ohio State community that facilitates creative and interdisciplinary collaboration, innovation, and dissemination. As a pilot, academic credit was not given, there was no fee to participate, and participants could drop in on sessions that interest them. The second year was augmented with a $10,000 budget from The Barnett Center, a $5000 grant from GCAC, and the creation of a special topics course. Participation was mandatory, 3 credit units were given to both undergraduate and graduate students who enrolled; Columbus artists had to register in advance but were not charged a fee to participate. The class was changed to a 4-week intensive and met Monday through Friday evenings May 10 to June 5, 2017. Dr Crum was the lead facilitator for both cohorts and imbedded into the curriculum sessions on mission statements, vision statements, and unique value propositions. Participants were able to articulate how the mission, vision, and the value offered to their customers laid the foundation for how to progress forward in business. Participants learn through hands-on activities and ongoing feedback from peers and professionals. What follows are the creative professionals the authors worked with to co-facilitate workshops in building skills in specific areas.

Branding and Marketing: Marshall Shorts is a graphic designer who helps artists learn that they are their brand. He is the founder of ARTfluential branding agency and co-founder of Creative Control Fest (CCF). ARTfluential helps business owners with small to mid-sized budgets spread their message to targeted audiences. CCF is an annual grassroots conference and festival with the goal to help grow an ethnically and culturally diverse landscape while providing exposure, resources, and opportunities in the design and creative fields. Shorts helped participants determine their audience, construct their message, and offer free and low-cost strategies to market their message to potential customers in order to increase profit.

Diverse Revenue Streams: Cynthia and Kevin Turner are a creative couple who shared how to create passive income. Dr Cynthia Turner is a CPA, author and professor of accounting and management information systems at OSU. Kevin Turner is an author and professional musician. Together they run a record label and have written and published books in their respective fields. They shared with participants how writing about their expertise in textbooks, blogs, and self-publishing can be a way to gain multiple streams of income for success.

Negotiation: Adam Brouillette is an artist, designer, and founder of Blockfort Studios. Brouillette discussed how a studio rental business can build a creative community and create sustainable income. He also shared best practices for artists to negotiate with clients, gallerists, and collectors in order to present their value to their market to receive the compensation they desire.

Copyrights and Contracts: Stefan "T.Wong" Thomas is a singer, songwriter, and co-founding attorney of Thomas Ingram Law Group. He shared how to evaluate contracts, the differences between copyrights and trademarks, and determine business' tax designations. Thomas identified basic legal strategies and lexicon for participants to keep their businesses protected.

Budgeting: Elaine Grogan Luttrull is a CPA, assistant professor, and department head of the Business and Entrepreneurship of Columbus College of Art and Design and founder of Minerva Financial Arts. She led participants through an interactive budgeting exercise to help them learn the importance of money management.

Putting it into Practice: The authors invited five arts-based business owners from different industries to share their creative entrepreneurial journeys. Dwight Heckelman is the founder of Groove U—a post-secondary school offering two-year degrees in music industry professions. Celeste Malvar-Stewart is the founder of Malvar = Stewart—an eco-conscious fashion company that uses salvaged fine vintage fabrics and wool from local farmers for women's clothes and accessories. Carnell Willoughby is the co-founder of Willowbeez Soulveg—a food business that seeks to change the local perception of health-conscious eating by providing a vegetarian spin on traditional African American and Caribbean dishes. Troy Stith is a 2016 AWS participant. Stith is a self-taught painter who shared his business plan and how AWS helped him gain additional skills in building his business. Louise Robinson, member of the Grammy Award-winning a cappella ensemble Sweet Honey in the Rock, shared how to remain relevant and profitable during a 40-year tenure in the music industry.

On the last day of the series, participants presented their business plan using the business model canvas—a visual outline of a business plan with nine critical components for leading a successful business: value proposition, customer segments, cost structure, revenue stream, customer relationships, distribution channels, key partners, key activities, and key resources. As the participants presented their business model canvas to the cohort and invited professionals, written feedback was given to each AWS presenter that focused specifically on their creative enterprise.

Conclusion

AWS supports emerging artists face their biggest challenge: Creating a business plan. Through community–university partnerships, the authors worked to support artists and creative students prepare to make their passion their profit. This type of partnership allows students to work with professional and emerging artists in their cohort, learn from active creative entrepreneurs, and create the potential for universities to reach alumni needing additional support to be successful after graduation. Maintaining diverse cohorts of community artists, students, and alumni is important for students to build networks and form collaborations while understanding the post academic reality of sustaining an arts career.

The uniqueness of this program is the community-university partnerships established between the local funding communities to meet the needs of Columbus based artists as well as OSU students and alumni. By combining resources from both the City of Columbus and OSU through The Barnett Center, an academic curriculum and practicum that met the needs of students, alumni, emerging, and professional artists was developed. Assessment of both cohorts is underway. In-depth interviews with 2016 cohort participants will be conducted to understand impact of the program one-year later. A survey of the 2017 cohort is being conducted to assess product design and implementation. Findings are expected to be released in Fall 2017.

A thank you note from one of the 2017 participants, a painter, and OSU alumnae, on her experience participating in the *ARTrepreneur Workshop Series* concisely states the objective for each participant,

> I want to thank you for the amazing opportunity to attend the *ARTrepreneur Workshop Series. It* was beyond a game changer... it's easy to justify it as a life changer. Because of this workshop I was able to refine my offerings, find my voice, understand my customers, overhaul my website, develop a marketing plan, re-price my work, develop new revenue streams, and create a three-year plan to become a full-time artist. Thank you and the Barnett Center for helping to make this OSU alumni dreams come true!

So many artists face challenges with starting a creative business. It is the duty of universities to ensure students are equipped with the knowledge to be successful. By collaborating with creative experts outside of the university, professors help their students take the courageous leap into ARTrepreneurship.

References

Clifford, C. 2013. "Artists are Job-Creating Entrepreneurs, Too." *Entrepreneur.* http://entrepreneur.com/article/230038 (accessed May 22, 2017).

Goodman, M. 2015. "10 Industries Benefiting From Incubators." *Entrepreneur.* http://entrepreneur.com/article/249510 (accessed May 22, 2017).

Wallace, N. 2016. "The Top Ten Cities for Creatives." *Smart Asset.* https://smartasset.com/mortgage/the-top-ten-cities-for-creatives (accessed May 22, 2017).

CHAPTER 8

Development of Performance-Based Class Projects in the Arts

Larry Stapleton and J. Mark Munoz

Universities have long understood the need to provide students with the opportunity to demonstrate their ability to apply the course content within the context of a real-world scenario. Kolb (1984) stressed the importance of experience in the process of learning. The best way to achieve this requires that faculty develop a client based project which is relevant to the course. Faculty have experienced difficulties in developing project based courses because of the complexities in identifying potential clients, linking the course content to the needs of the client and determining how to measure the level of success in meeting the client's expectations.

Most real-world projects require discussion between the client and the project team to evolve the objectives of the project and develop an integrative solution. The lack of project objectives clarity is due to the client's initial ambiguity regarding the desired outcome and the project teams limited understanding of the relevant industry. Various literature suggest that hands-on learning can make a difference in business. For instance, competencies in business functions is essential in entrepreneurial education (Barringer and Ireland 2011). Competencies can be improved with training (Klarus, Tillema, and Veenstra 1999). Action is the foundation of entrepreneurship (McMullen and Shepherd 2006).

In addition, universities strive to promote the globalization of student experiences by asking faculty to consider the implications of global factors within the development of a project solution. Katula and Threnhauser

(1999) indicated that overseas studies are a form of experiential education. International student projects in arts entrepreneurship offers unique ways for students to learn.

The advantages perceived by faculty to demonstrate course content via a global project are balanced by the perceived added logistical and cultural complexities in developing such a course.

The focus of this paper is to discuss the factors to consider in developing a client based project, the complexities added by implementing a global project, and the metrics to consider in determining success. The paper will include examples of global projects conducted as part of a Doing Business in the Dominican Republic class at Millikin University. The focus of these global projects is the promotion of entrepreneurship within the arts community in the Dominican Republic. The examples will include lessons learned on pedagogy, development of a client base and logistics of a travel based course.

Considerations in Developing an International Arts and Entrepreneurship Course

Development of a Client Base

One daunting task of a client based project is how to find clients who wish to participate. Business and art students are told about the importance of networking but many faculty have difficulty in developing and utilizing their networks. The reasons can relate to the perceived limitations of their network, a limited understanding of what their network offers and a perception that it is an imposition on their colleagues. These perceptions on networking are mostly unfounded. By making needs known, often times allows client opportunities to emerge. The issue is being prepared to know how to utilize the opportunity in the class. One of the simplest approaches is to stay in contact and let networks know topics of interest and letting others know of past project accomplishments. Using social media such as Linkedin, blogs, Twitter, and Facebook are excellent ways of letting people know about current research focus and past project successes. One key issue is the required time to keep social media outlets current. This updating takes time and must be directed in a purposeful manner.

Potential sources for identifying clients:

- Academic conferences, associations, and clubs.
- Federal, state and local government agencies can be another fruitful source of projects.
- The Chamber of Commerce is a potential source for local, state and international projects.
- Most U.S. embassies have a Trade Attaché whose role is to promote US trade in the host country.
- Local industries in the community
- Community Arts Councils, community theater companies, Local cultural organizations, community music and symphony guilds, and so on.

The key to success is to adopt a proactive follow up approach to conversations on potential projects.

Relationship to Course Content

A typical university level course has multiple objectives. A faculty member will likely structure the course to meet the objectives relative to a perceived level of importance. The inclusion of a client based project may require the prioritization of the class objectives to meet the client's needs. Thus, a client based project may require a change from the previous course structure. Some may wonder whether the project should drive the direction of the course or should the course drive the direction of the project. The criterion for selecting a specific project should not be based solely on availability nor should it be on its match with previous pedagogy. Being open to changes in the pedagogy used to meet course objectives, is central to the selection of client based projects. Successful use of client based projects to accomplish course objectives can only be achieved when faculty have clarity on the essence of the course.

Client based projects requires students to move outside of their "comfort zone." The integrative nature of client based projects requires the student to draw upon multiple skills and new areas of knowledge. Client based projects require both the student and the faculty to be fearless and adopt a "why not" versus a "why should we" approach to meeting a course objective.

The multifunctional nature of decision making can be incorporated into the project by collaborating with other courses, both within and outside of the faculty and student area of expertise. The inclusion of courses outside the student's area of expertise promotes team building and how to seek out, analyze and incorporate information in the project solution.

International Influences

The internationalization of a project can provide immense benefits in terms of exposure to experiences beyond the student's current comprehension to the challenge of creating a more realistic solution (Rambler 1991). However, the inclusion of a global influence to a project brings added challenges especially if it includes a travel component. The challenges include local customs and cultural differences, language barrier, transportation logistics, accommodation preferences, dietary considerations, to name a few. These challenges can impact both the student perceptions on the value of the experience and the client's perception of the project's success. The authors' personal experience is that these challenges prevent faculty from considering the inclusion of travel component as they do not know how to address these concerns. The logistical and pedagogical complexities of implementing an international travel course are discussed in the lessons learned segment of this paper. Many university curriculums require the students to read about cultural differences but it is only abstract concepts until the student experiences it in action.

Learning from Successes and Failures: International Student Projects in Arts Entrepreneurship

Millikin University has offered a course titled Doing Business in the Dominican Republic (DR) since 2011. The course has evolved over time to adjust to the clients' needs and the expansion of the local network in the Dominican Republic. The class focused on exploring solutions for projects which impacted Dominican artists. These projects have ranged from developing ways to finance local artists to development of an entrepreneurship hub with an Arts emphasis. Participation has varied from 12 to 18 students per course with the majority being junior and senior business, nursing, fine arts and arts and science majors, with the majority being business majors. The intentional and cognizant approach of recruiting students across multiple disciplines provided value due to the different approaches of developing solutions, providing benefit to the course and the client.

The inaugural class focused on how to create a microfinance fund focusing on women artists in the Dominican Republic. The course structure required the students to meet with faculty a few times in a traditional classroom setting prior to traveling to the Dominican Republic for eight days. The focus was to gather information for the development of a business plan for a new student organization titled the Millikin Microfinance Fund (MMF). The travel component was essential as a source of secondary research on women artists in the Dominican Republic. Using online databases and interviewing faculty who had traveled to the Dominican Republic, provided little information. The research identified a single point of contact based on discussions with other business and education faculty which had visited the Dominican Republic four or five years previously. In addition, the online research identified an obscure startup magazine, La Lengua, which focused on local art and related cultural events. The founders of La Lengua were alumni of the art school Altos de Chavon. They studied drawing, sculpture and painting. The focus of the magazine was to promote art, not arts and crafts. The publishers tried to develop a means by which other alumni of art schools could show their work, discuss current trends and promote the business aspects of the art world. The Millikin group learned much about the struggles which local artists faced in marketing their art.

Operational Learning Points

The initial trip had multiple objectives: (1) explore the needs of the art community in the Dominican Republic, primarily women artists with entrepreneurial intent; (2) discuss microfinance structure and opportunities with a local microfinance organization; and (3) acclimatize the faculty in the logistics and cultural differences that would be involved with a project based course.

This initial trip taught the faculty and students the following about international operations:

1. A client based course could not be satisfactorily completed during a two-week immersion course.
2. The focus of the microfinance project needed to be redefined to women entrepreneurs, with a preference to be given to artists.
3. For the microfinance project to be successful it needed to partner with a local microfinance organization which knew the locals, had a selection process and a collection process already developed.
4. Faculty started a database which included accommodations, restaurants, local cultural sites and transportation which meet the expectations of the students.
5. Faculty explored the balance between emphasizing the need for students to spend the time to create a viable solution with the need to make this experience enjoyable.

International Research Learning Points

The second course focused on the implementation of the microfinance business plan and lessons learned from the first trip. The course structure changed from an immersion course to a ten-week course offered in the Fall semester. The faculty identified several potential partners which had existing local support structures and a network of local entrepreneurs. The focus was to develop a method to interview and select a partner, with the intent of signing a contract during an in-country visit. The groups were broken up by potential partners for due diligence purposes. The selection method identified included financial stability, extensiveness of network, potential return on investment, how well they could implement the strategic intent of loaning to women artists. The group followed up with the La Lingua team, only to find out the magazine had folded. The La Lengua team shared some lessons learned and what they were considering for future projects.

In this experience, faculty and students learned about international research and cross-cultural activities:

1. Even an expansion of the course to allow students to perform more in-depth research and explore new possible solutions did not fully remove the ambiguities of a client based project.
2. Technology in the form of emails, phone calls and even Skype did not fully address the students' questions, which could only be answered during the international travel part of the course.
3. Students enjoy learning about the cultural and historical aspects of country.

Management Learning Points

The faculty's work with the microfinance project expanded to include a new project by the La Lengua team. The La Lengua team determined that local artists needed a space to interface with their peers, hold meetings with potential clients and to learn about marketing their art. The year's trip held a dual purpose which included the evaluation of the microfinance fund success and working with the group of local artists developing an entrepreneurship hub in Santo Domingo. The student group was divided into smaller teams to work with La Lengua to develop a marketing plan, an organizational structure, pricing schedule, potential arts related business courses and an initial budget. Though the students had developed each of these business plan components in previous courses using case studies and textbook exercises, they found that working with a client was different. The faculty and students learned the following about management:

1. Gathering information by listening was much different than by reading. If one did not understand a certain point in a case study, assumptions would be made. If client comments are not understood, one can ask for clarification.
2. Client objectives can be conflicting.
3. Client preferred solutions may be based on satisfying a singular objective.
4. Interview questions need to seek client's intent as well as content.
5. How the solution is presented to the client is important in gaining acceptance.

Arts and Entrepreneurship Learning Points

The following year, the faculty expanded relationships to include the school from which the La Lengua team graduated, La Escuela de Diseno Altos de Chavon. The school has been identified as one of the 13 best design schools in the world. The school provides instruction in the areas of communication design, fashion design, fine arts, illustration, digital design, interior design, photography, film production, and architecture. The school is located in a resort community which limits access primarily to guests, homeowners and tourists from cruise lines. It had a renowned faculty and produce skilled artists that exhibit select works in an on-site gallery. The course focus was to explore ways to promote both student and faculty work through the development of a website, involvement with tourism outside the resort community and promotion to the resort's upscale clientele. The faculty and students continued involvement with the microfinance project by refining contracts and focus on fund recipients. Faculty and student lessons regarding arts and entrepreneurship included the following:

1. Limited knowledge in a technical area should not prevent exploring an opportunity. No one in the group had experience in developing a website. But by seeking expert help and perseverance the group created a professional grade website.
2. To be successful, it is important to know who the decision maker is on the client side. Though the website was enthusiastically received by the client, it was later uncovered that the client was not the final decision maker. This resulted in an extensive delay in its implementation.
3. A successful solution needs to be of sufficient detail regarding timeline, resource needs and budget. Groups that presented general ideas without the detail were not received well by the client. The client wants to know the how, the who, how much and how long.
4. Students learned that the valuation of an item especially art is very subjective. The student art pricing schedule presented by the tourist marketing group was not in line with the value defined by the artist.

Developing and Presenting a Solution Learning Points

The contacts faculty and students made with members of the local art and cultural community in the city of La Romana through the school formed the basis for the year's projects. Working with the Provincial Director of Culture of La Romana led to the identification of several other potential projects. These projects included development of a strategic plan for a new cultural center which was being transformed from an infamous local prison. The projects included how to market to locals and tourists, providing master classes for local artists, and development of relationships with international partners. The work with La Escuela de Diseno Altos de Chavon continued with the exploration of ways to find opportunities to market student work. The learning points were as follows:

1. The development of actions in the absence of a strategic plan that is accepted at all levels makes it difficult to develop a viable plan.
2. The students discovered the need to understand the organizational chart and who is responsible for making the final decision.
3. The acceptable time to accomplish a task can vary and is related to cultural norms.
4. Look for solutions which may require inclusions of partnerships which complement the skills of the local organization.
5. To create a meaningful solution requires an understanding of where the local organization is in achieving their current objectives, past solutions tried and what level of achievement is sought.

Recommendations for International Projects in Arts and Entrepreneurship

The authors' experience in developing international client based projects with an arts and entrepreneurship focus may help in the development of similar projects in arts education.

Consider cultural implications. It has been well documented that the internationalization of a project requires the participants to respect cultural differences. What one person believes is important does not mean that others share that belief. This statement is applicable when the client is of a different nationality or a different mindset. Cultural differences were found across multiple projects in the Dominican Republic. Different cultural mindsets were noticed between the business students and the clients with artistic backgrounds. The timelines for project completion promoted by the business students and the clients varied. The mindset on the value of a piece of art was viewed differently between the students and the client, even where the subjectivity of the pricing was considered.

Socialize and communicate clearly. The development of a network, which began with one person, was the result of successful communication, wishes of past clients, people clients knew and sources outside both networks. When expanding a network, there will be other parties who will think that efforts placed are self-benefiting only. It is, therefore important to make sure that faculty and students express capabilities clearly and that intentions are well articulated and highlight benefits to the client.

Adapt and build efficiencies. Success can be found by building on the work of other's previous efforts. "Do not try not to reinvent the wheel." If other projects are successful in a geographic region or in an academic area outside one's expertise, then consider ways where past lessons learned can be adapted to the new project. An important approach is to provide an experience for the students to apply course content. The benefits can include adaption of a project, knowledge about the geographic region, contact and logistics such as hotel and transportation costs.

Find strategic partners. Seek out partners who may have complementary objectives and knowledge. The projects included efforts to collaborate with other programs such as: nursing, education, entrepreneurship and fine arts.

Offer out-of-the-box learning. Most students do not have the confidence to develop a solution which they feel will be meaningful to the client. The typical responses concerns collected from students who participated in the projects included: (1) lack of industry experience; (2) lack of experience with defining client expectations; (3) lack of experience working with ambiguous objectives; (4) fear of working outside comfort zone; and (5) most solutions require and integrative approach using content learned in multiple classes. The authors found the need to develop teams which have complementary strengths. Seeking out and partnering with experts in fields outside their own helped students reduce their knowledge gap, analyze key data and review solutions from different perspectives.

Focus on value. Present information that not only meets the needs of the client but also presented in a format which is understandable and direct. Some students want to do a data dump and provide both relevant and irrelevant data. By working with the client, the students learned the importance of presenting in terms of what the client could relate to in actions, resources and measurements for success.

Make students the "stars." Faculty need to allow students to learn their own way, and present their solutions, not those of the faculty. The authors were acutely aware that the success of the current project may impact the ability of the faculty to work on future projects with the client. The question of how to guide, versus dictate, the students to a potential solution was present in every project. Setting the bar at a high level at the very beginning helped in this regard. Constant reminder of expectations and accountability was helpful. But, ultimately, helping the students shine and run their own show led to very positive results.

Undertaking an international client based project focused on arts and entrepreneurship is a challenge. Nevertheless, the benefits are significant to both faculty and students. All participants must go in to the project with a positive and fearless mindset in seeking to accomplish at most times an ambiguous effort. Considering the increasing interest in arts and entrepreneurship and its growing practice worldwide, merging academic and practical experiences could be an effective way to groom the next generation of artists and prepare them for professional success.

References

Barringer, B.R., and R.D. Ireland. 2011. *Entrepreneurship: Successfully Launching New Ventures*, 4th ed. Boston: Prentice Hall.

Katula, R., and E. Threnhauser. 1999. Experiential Education in the Undergraduate Curriculum. *Communication Education* 48, pp. 238–55.

Klarus, R., H. Tillema, and J. Veenstra. 1999. "Beoordelen: Met Competentieprofielen of Kwalificatiestructuren: Onderwijs en Bedrijfsleven Staan Weliswaar nog ver van Elkaar af in de Wijze Waarop zij Beoordelen, Maar Groeien Meer en Meer naar Elkaar toe in Denken over en Kiezen van de Wijze van Beoordeling van Medewerkers." *Opleiding and Ontwikkeling* 12, no. 11, pp. 15–26.

Kolb, D. 1984. *Experiential Learning: Experience as the Source of Learning and Development,* 20–38. Englewood Cliffs, NJ: Prentice-Hall.

McMullen, J., and D. Shepherd. 2006. "Entrepreneurial Action and the Role of Uncertainty in the Theory of the Entrepreneur." *Academy of Management Review* 31, pp. 132–152.

CHAPTER 9

Strategic Entrepreneurship in Self-Employment in the Arts

Robert Moussetis

The artistic masterpieces created by Michelangelo were supported by vision, planning capabilities, coordinating skills, maintained flow of necessary resources, networking, and engagement in public relations (Wallace 1994). All these activities are descriptive of a couple of characteristics: Strategy and Entrepreneurship. Michelangelo was self-employed!

Considering that the majority of the work in Self-Employment in the Arts is project oriented, the majority of the research focuses on two areas: *educating the artist* in entrepreneurship (Bauer, Viola and Strauss 2011; Murugesan and Jayavelu 2015; Gangi 2015; Thom 2017; Welsh, Onishi, DeHoog, and Syed 2014; Essig 2013; Shockley and Frank 2013; White 2013; Bridgstock 2013; Bonin-Rodriguez 2012; Preece 2011) or *specific topics in a variety of artistic areas* (Lord 2012; Nytch 2012; Mathew and Carl 2013; Kolsteeg 2013; Pollard and Wilson 2014; Preece 2014; Webb 2014; Enhuber 2014; Sacco, Blessi, and Nuccio 2009; Besana and Clavenna 2012; Kuhn and Galloway 2015; Abfalter 2013), including arts entrepreneurship definition (Swedberg 2006).

In addressing these two main areas, it is suggested to create a conceptual model that provides a guiding tool for artists that develops both their artistic craft while being strategic and entrepreneurial. In addition, there are three major characteristics in the strategic and entrepreneurial success of an artist: the ability to identify societal (cultural) shifts, artists' entrepreneurial behavior, and capability.

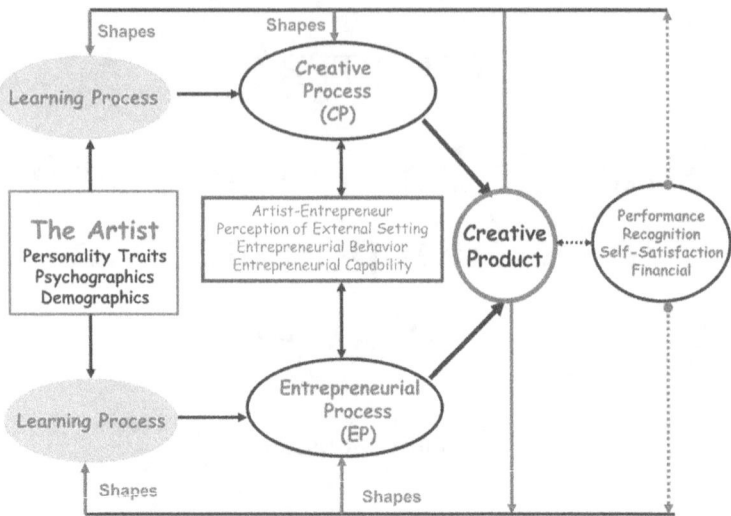

Figure 9.1 The entrepreneurial self-employed artist

Brief context of the conceptual model: The conceptual model presented here (Figure 9.1) serves as a conceptual map to facilitate the development of the contextual setting of the Entrepreneurial Self-Employed Artist. It also provides a launching pad for future empirical research addressing assessment of societal shifts, entrepreneurial orientation, ability to respond in conjunction to learning, personality traits, and performance.

Brief model description: The top part refers to the artistic creation; this model is introducing the entrepreneurial part as an integral part of the success (performance). The degree of success shapes future changes, both artistic and entrepreneurial. The personality characteristics will shape the learning process which results in the creation of the aesthetic product in conjunction with the business of art (selling and making a living or even getting rich). Simultaneously, the external perceptions maintained by an artist, entrepreneurial behavior, and capability will shape the creative and entrepreneurial efforts leading to an aesthetic "product." Certainly, such characteristics play a role in the success of their aesthetic expression. Success, though, needs to be defined in multiple ways (rewards, satisfaction, recognition, etc.). Success will shape future (trial and error, failures) artistic/entrepreneurial activities leading to a self-feeding cycle of growth.

Contextual Background

Artist as self-employed entrepreneur: The question arises whether artists have similar characteristics as traditionally perceived entrepreneurs. Most entrepreneurs expect lower initial earnings (Astebro and Chen 2014; Hyytinen, Ilmakunnas, and Toivanen 2013; Hamilton 2000); their relevant experience and training indicates a higher degree of success (Jones-Evans 1996; Vesper 1992), and age favors younger entrepreneurs than older (Croft and Dickinson 1988). Increasingly, the art education literature investigates multiculturalism, gender and race (DelaCruz 2003; Wagner-Ott 2002), expanding definition of art education and paradigmic shifts (Kamhi 2003), and importance of art education (Kindler 2003; Barbosa 1991; Duncum 1990, 2001; Garoian 1997; McFee and Degge 1977; Neperud 1995; Tavin 2001; Wilson 2001). It is apparent that professional artists are required to develop in-depth business experience to couple the artistic flair (Bolan 2002) and perhaps to build bridges both intellectual and pragmatic to erase the perception that artists are from Mars and business persons are from Venus (Boyle and Weight 2002).

Personality: Humans perform well when there is a fit between personality type and the characteristics of the environment. Lack of similarity between personality and environment leads to un-fulfillment. (Loveland et al. 2016; Holland 1996; Schneider 1987; Schneider, Goldstein, and Smith 1995; Kelloway et al. 2010). Previous research on entrepreneurship has focused on personality characteristics as a predictor of entrepreneurial orientation (Obschonka, Silbereisen, and Schmitt-Rodermund 2012; Schmitt-Rodermund 2007; Carland et al. 1984) and behavioral elements (Lumpkin and Dess 1996). As entrepreneurs search for unfilled needs, innovative approaches to serve existing markets, similarly, artists are searching for a niche that will give them an aesthetic distinction.

Behavior: The nature of artistic work implies that the core behavior of an artist is associated with their craft; nevertheless, since artists must make a living, they often display behavior ranges from entrepreneurial to bohemian (Lindstrom 2016). Moreover, does entrepreneurial education relates to entrepreneurial behavioral (Rauch and Hulsink 2015)? If accepting the postulation that entrepreneurship is closely associated with greater risks, it is logical to explore the entrepreneurial behavior theory to investigate behavioral parallels between entrepreneurs and artists. It is suggested that artistic entrepreneurial behavior will define the dynamics affecting an artist and their work.

Learning and knowledge: Entrepreneurial learning is a product of experience and/or knowledge (Castellaneta and Conti 2017; Reuber and Fischer 1994; Reuber, Dyke, and Fischer 1990) or even impulse (Minnit and Bygrave 2001) based on experimentation and past successes. Hence, there is a self-reinforcing learning component that continues to drive entrepreneurial activities (Minnit and Bygrave 2000; Kolb 1984). Similarly, artists engage in projects based on knowledge or impulse and the artists' previous success/failures feeds (learning process) future projects. Therefore, it can be assumed that artists also learn from experience and/or knowledge. Traditional entrepreneurship and learning is associated with the capability to recognize opportunities (Ronstadt 1988; Shane and Venkataraman 2000) and learning how to overcome difficulties (Aldrich 1999; Shepherd, Douglas, and Shanley 2000). For an artist, the opportunity is within an existing market (incremental art) or engaging in a new form of aesthetic expression as traditional entrepreneurs innovate and introduce novel products with high degree of uncertainty. Most artists will engage in established aesthetics domains (rock music, wedding photography, commercial acting) and a few are engaging into new aesthetic domains (i.e., rock music in late 50s early 60s, digital animation in the 90s, etc.).

Typologies of entrepreneurial behavior of artists: In borrowing from the vast managerial and entrepreneurial behavioral theory, intuitively, there are typologies to suggest behavioral characteristics of artists. Two types of behavioral approaches are suggested: **Incremental and Novel**

> **Incremental:** Art relating to past work-repetitive-slightly different but never radically new
> **Novel-creative:** Art not relating to past work-seeking novel new artistic angles

Understandably, some artists will fall into both categories but most earn a living by identifying with either incremental or novel art. For example, music teachers may consider themselves as artists, however, unless they are writing and playing novel music one may argue that, at best, they are incremental artists (minor changes or repetitive work over time) while a novel musician is constantly writing new music and exploring different dimensions of her/his artistic skill. The management literature suggests that behaviors and capabilities must match the intensity of the external environment. For example, if the environment is highly unpredictable, complex, and/or fast changing, then the appropriate behavior is entrepreneurial and creative (miles and Snow 1978; Ansoff and Sullivan 1993); artists tend to have such behaviors and capabilities almost by default (their work is project oriented—Eickoff, 2013). However, there are some artists that like repetitive work (teaching music to young adults or wedding photography) where changes are slow with the ability to change based on past work and/or experience.

Therefore, Tables 9.1 and 9.2 represent a practical guide for self-employed artists to examine whether their entrepreneurial orientation and ability to respond matches the societal shifts. Table 9.1 represents the ideal scenario where the self-employed artist is matching entrepreneurial orientation and ability to change to external societal and cultural changes where Table 9.2 represents a suboptimal scenario. In Table 9.2 the gap level between the external environment and entrepreneurial orientation and ability to change is 2 (Gap = 2). The bigger the gap the more suboptimal performance will be displayed by the self-employed artist (Ansoff and Sullivan 1993).

So What? The model provides a launch pad for artists and academicians to investigate the degree of entrepreneurship (if any) applied by artists. It provides a start for a discussion to systematically analyze and institutionalize this emerging field; most importantly, it will provide artists with mechanisms to actively think of the entrepreneurial part of their craft. The tables are a practical guide to operationalize their entrepreneurial work based on the societal shifts. Naturally, this research effort rendered an axiomatic reference that artists are interested in financial betterment of their individual lives. The operating assumption is that the

Table 9.1 *Optimal scenario*

External environment	Repetitive	Repetitive scale based	Changing self-promotions	Entrepreneurial	Creativity
	1	2	3	4	5
Levels of societal shifts and cultural changes					
Speed, predictability and complexity of changes	Repetitive	Expanding Slow incremental	Changing Fast incremental	Discontinuous Predictable	Surprising Unpredictable
Entrepreneurial orientation	Seeks stability	Reacts to changes	Anticipates changes	Entrepreneurial	Creative
Entrepreneurial approach	Based on previous work	Incremental Based on experience	Incremental Based on extrapolation	Discontinuous Based on expected futures	Discontinuous Based on creativity
Ability to respond to changes	Suppresses changes	Adapts to Change	Pursues familiar change	Seeks new changes	Seeks novel changes

Table 9.2 *Suboptimal scenario*

External environment	Repetitive	Repetitive scale based	Changing self-promotions	Entrepreneurial	Creativity
Levels of societal shifts and cultural changes	1	2	3	4	5
Speed, predictability and complexity of changes	Repetitive	Expanding Slow Incremental	Changing Fast incremental	Discontinuous Predictable	Surprising Unpredictable
Entrepreneurial orientation	Seeks stability	Reacts to changes	Anticipates changes	Entrepreneurial	Creative
Entrepreneurial Approach	Based on previous work	Incremental Based on experience	Incremental Based on extrapolation	Discontinuous Based on expected futures	Discontinuous Based on creativity
Ability to respond to changes	Suppresses changes	Adapts to change	Pursues familiar change	Seeks new change	Seeks novel change

great majority of artists hope for enough artistic and financial success to earn an adequate and secure financial living.

Conclusion: Aspiring artists generally have a broad understanding of the risks associated with the arts but do not have a clear professional or business plan. Their passion of art is the driving force behind their choices. However, without the tools to recognize the external shifts as they relate to a corresponding entrepreneurial orientation and ability to change, creates additional challenges. Moreover, this model provides a holistic conceptual view that allows artists to view all the critical factors simultaneously (proper skills and knowledge to create marketable product). It is my belief that artists are unsystematic entrepreneurs. This research effort is an attempt to provide a more systematic approach to the artistic craft. The Arts and Entrepreneurship field is "brewing" with research and programs across the country. This emerging field will create a new body of artists along with the growing number of educators who recognize the important association between business and art.

Bibliography

Abfalter, D. 2013. "Authenticity and Respect: Leading Creative Teams in the Performing Arts." *Creativity and Innovation Management* 22, no. 3, pp. 295–306

Aldrich, H. 1999. *Organizations Evolving.* London: Sage.

Ansoff, I.H., and P.A. Sullivan. 1993. "Optimizing Profitability in Turbulent Environments: A Formula for Strategic Success." *Long Range Planning* 26, pp.11–23.

Astebro, T., and J. Chen. 2014. "The Entrepreneurial Earnings Puzzle: Mismeasurement or Real?" *Journal of Business Venturing* 29, no. 1, pp. 88–105.

Barbosa, A.M. 1991. "Art Education and Environment." *Journal of Multicultural and Cross Cultural Research in Art Education* 9, no. 1, pp. 59–64.

Bauer, C., K. Viola, and C. Strauss. 2011. "Management Skills for Artists: 'Learning by Doing'?" *International Journal of Cultural Policy* 17, no. 5, pp. 626–44.

Besana, A., and V. Clavenna. 2012. "Advertising and Branding of Italian Visual Arts at 'Hard Times.'" *The International Conference on Applied Economics (ICOAE)* 1, 41–50. Uppsala, Sweden, 2012, Procedia Economics and Finance.

Bonin-Rodriguez, P. 2012. "What's in a Name? Typifying Artist Entrepreneurship in Community Based Training." *Artivate: A Journal of Entrepreneurship in the Arts* 1, no. 1, pp. 9–24.

Bridgstock, R. 2013. "Not a Dirty Word: Arts Entrepreneurship and Higher Education." *Arts and Humanities in Higher Education* 12, nos. 2–3, pp. 122–37.

Boyle, L., and M. Weight. 2002. "The Age Old Argument." *Target Marketing* 25, no. 3 pp. 38–42.

Bolan, S. 2002. "Artists Need Business Know-How." *Computing Canada* 28, no. 7, p. 19.

Carland, J.W., F. Hoy, W.R. Boulton, and J.A.C. Carland. 1984. "Differentiating Entrepreneurs from Small Business Owners." *Academy of Management Review* 9, no. 2, pp. 354–59.

Castellaneta, F., and R. Conti. 2017. "How Does Acquisition Experience Create Value? Evidence from a Regulatory Change Affecting the Information Environment." *European Management Journal* 31, no. 1, pp. 60–68.

Croft, N.L., and D. Dickinson. 1988. "To be Young and in Business." *Nation's Business* 76, no. 3, pp. 63–65.

Delacruz, E.M. 2003. "Racism American Style and Resistance to Change: Art Education's Role in the Indian Mascot Issue." *Art Education* 56, no. 5, pp. 13–20.

Duncum, P. 1990. "Clearing the Decks for Dominant Culture: A Contemporary Art Education." *Studies in Art Education* 31, no. 4, pp. 207–15.

Dyke, L.S., E.M. Fischer, and A.R. Reuber. 1992. "An Inter-Industry Examination of the Impact of the Owner Experience on Firm Performance." *Journal of Small Business Management* 30, no. 4, pp. 72–87

Eikhof, D.R., and A. Haunschild. 2007. "For Art's Sake! Artistic and Economic Logics in Creative Production." *Journal of Organizational Behavior* 28, pp. 523–38.

Enhuber, M. 2014. "How is Damien Hirst a Cultural Entrepreneur?" *Artivate: A Journal of Entrepreneurship in the Arts* 3, no. 2, pp. 3–20.

Essig, L. 2013. "Frameworks for Educating the Artist of the Future: Teaching Habits of Mind for Arts Entrepreneurship." *Artivate: A Journal of Entrepreneurship in the Arts* 1, no. 2, pp. 65–78.

Garoian, C.R. 1997. "Art education and the Aesthetics of Health in the Age of AIDS." *Studies in Art Education* 39, no. 1, pp. 6–23.

Gangi, J. 2015. "The Synergies of Artistic and Entrepreneurial Action." *Journal of Arts Management, Law & Society* 45, no. 4, pp. 247–54.

Hamilton, B.H. 2000. "Does Entrepreneurship Pay? An Empirical Analysis of the Returns to Self-Employment." *Journal of Political Economy* 108, no. 3, pp. 604–31.

Holland, J.L. 1996. "Exploring Careers with a Typology: What We have Learned and Some New Directions." *American Psychologist* 51, no. 4, pp. 397–406.

Hyytinen, A., P. Ilmakunnas, and O. Toivanen. 2013. "The Returns to Entrepreneurship Puzzle." *Labour Economics* 20, pp. 57–67.

Jones-Evans, D. 1996. "Technical Entrepreneurship, Strategy and Experience." *International Small Business Journal* 14, no. 3, pp. 15–39.

Kelloway, K.E., L. Francis, M. Prosser, and J.E. Cameron. 2010. "Counter productive Work Behavior as Protest." *Human Resource Management Review* 20, no. 1, pp. 18–25.

Kindler, A.M. 2003. "Visual Culture, Visual Brain, and (Art) Education." *Studies in Art Education* 44, no. 3, pp. 290–96.

Kolsteeg, J. 2013. "Situated Cultural Entrepreneurship." *Artivate: A Journal of Entrepreneurship in the Arts* 2, no. 3, pp. 3–13.

Kolb, D.A. 1984. *Experiential Learning: Experience as the Source of Learning and Development.* Englewood Cliffs, NJ: Prentice Hall.

Kuhn, K.M., and T.L. Galloway. 2015. "With a Little Help from My Competitors: Peer Networking Among Artisan Entrepreneurs." *Entrepreneurship Theory and Practice* 39, no. 3, pp. 571–600.

Lindström, S. 2016. "Artists and Multiple Job Holding—Breadwinning Work as Mediating Between Bohemian and Entrepreneurial Identities and Behavior." *Nordic Journal of Working Life Studies* 6, no. 3, pp. 43–58.

Loveland, K.E., J.M. Loveland, J.W. Lounsbury, and D.C. Dantas. 2016. "A Portrait of the Artist as an Employee: The Impact of Personality on Career Satisfaction." *International Journal of Arts Management* 19, no. 1, pp. 4–15.

Lord, C. 2012. "Shattering the Myth of the Passive Spectator: Entrepreneurial Efforts to Define and Enhance Participation in 'Non-Participatory' Art." *Artivate: A Journal of Entrepreneurship in the Arts* 1, no. 1, pp. 35–49.

Lumpkin, G.T., and G.G. Dess. 1996. "Clarifying the Entrepreneurial Orientation Construct and Linking it to Performance." *Academy of Management Review* 21, no. 1, pp. 135–72.

Mathew, V., and P. Carl. 2013. "Culture Coin: A Commons-Based, Complementary Currency for the Arts and Its Impact on Scarcity, Virtue, Ethics, and the Imagination." *Artivate: A Journal of Entrepreneurship in the Arts* 2, no. 3, pp. 14–27.

McFee, J.K., and R. Degge. 1977. *Art, Culture, and Environment.* Belmont, CA: Wadsworth.

Miles, R.A., and C.C. Snow. 1978. *Organizational Strategy, Structure and Process.* New York: McGraw-Hill.

Minniti, M., and W. Bygrave. 2001. "A Dynamic Model of ET&P Entrepreneurial Learning." *Entrepreneurship Theory and Practice* 25, no. 3, pp. 5–16.

Murugesan, R., and R. Jayavelu. 2015. "Testing the Impact of Entrepreneurship Education on Business, Engineering and Arts and Science Students Using the Theory of Planned Behaviour: A Comparative Study." *Journal of Entrepreneurship in Emerging Economies* 7, no. 3, pp. 256–75.

Neperud, R.W. (Ed.). 1995. *Content and Community in Art and Visual Culture Education: Beyond Postmodernism.* New York & London: Teachers College Press.

Nytch, J. 2012. "The Case of the Pitsburg New Music Ensemble: An Illustration of Entrepreneurial Theory in an Artistic Setting." *Artivate: A Journal of Entrepreneurship in the Arts* 16, no. 2, pp. 42–52.

Obschonka, M., R.K. Silbereisen, and E. Schmitt-Rodermund. 2012. "Explaining Entrepreneurial Behavior: Dispositional Personality Traits, Growth of Personal Entrepreneurial Resources, and Business Idea Generation." *The Career Development Quarterly* 60, pp. 178–90.

Olson, P. 1985. "Entrepreneurship: Opportunistic Decision Makers." *Journal of Small Business Management* 11, no. 2, pp. 25–31.

Preece, S.B. 2014. "Social Bricolage in Arts Entrepreneurship: Building a Jazz Society from Scratch." *Artivate: A Journal of Entrepreneurship in the Arts* 3, no. 1, pp. 23–34.

Preece, S.B. 2011. "Performing Arts Entrepreneurship: Toward a Research Agenda." *The Journal of Arts Management, Law, and Society* 41, no. 2, pp. 103–20.

Pollard, V., and E. Wilson. 2014. "The 'Entrepreneurial Mindset' in Creative and Performing Arts Higher Education in Australia." *Artivate: A Journal of Entrepreneurship in the Arts* 3, no. 1, pp. 3–22.

Rauch, A., and W. Hulsink. 2015. "Putting Entrepreneurship Education Where the Intention to Act Lies: An Investigation Into the Impact of Entrepreneurship Education on Entrepreneurial Behavior." *Academy of Management Learning & Education* 14, no. 2, pp. 187–204.

Reuber, A.R., L.S. Dyke, and E.M. Fischer. 1990. "Experiential Acquired Knowledge and Entrepreneurial Success." Academy of *Management Best Paper Proceedings,* pp. 69–70.

Reuber, A.R., and E.M. Fischer. 1994. "Entrepreneur's Experience, Expertise and the Performance of Technology Based Firms." *IEEE Transaction of Engineering Management* 441, no. 4, pp. 365–74.

Ronstadt, R. 1988. "The Corridor Principle." *Journal of Business Venturing* 3, no. 1, pp. 31–40.

Sacco, P.L., G.T. Blessi, and M. Nuccio. 2009. "Cultural Policies and Local Planning Strategies: What Is the Role of Culture in Local Sustainable Development?" *Journal of Arts Management, Law & Society* 39, no. 1, pp. 45–64.

Schmitt-Rodermund, E. 2007. "The Long Way to Entrepreneurship: Personality, Parenting, Early Interests, and Competencies as Precursors for Entrepreneurial Activity Among the 'Termites.'" In *Approaches to Positive Youth Development,* eds. R.K. Silbereisen and R.M. Lerner, 205–24.

Shockley, G.E., and P.M. Frank. 2013. "Dostoevsky's 'The Grand Inquistor': Adding an Ethical Component to the Teaching of Non-Market Entrepreneurship." *Artivate: A Journal of Entrepreneurship in the Arts* 1, no. 2, pp. 79–91.

Schneider, B. 1987. "The People Make the Place." *Personnel Psychology* 40, no. 3, pp. 437–53.

Schneider, B., H.W. Goldstein, and D.B. Smith. 1995. "The ASA Framework: An Update." *Personnel Psychology* 48, no. 4, pp. 747–73.

Shane, S., and S. Venkataraman. 2000. "The Promise of Entrepreneurship as a Field of Research." *The Academy of Management Review* 25, no. 1, pp. 217–26.

Shepherd, D.A., E.J. Douglas, and M. Shanley. 2000. "New Venture Survival: Ignorance, External Shocks, and Risk Reduction Strategies." *Journal of Business Venturing* 15, nos. 5/6, pp. 393–410.

Stern, G.M. 1998. "Young Entrepreneurs make their Mark." *Nation's Business* 84, no. 8, pp. 49–51.

Swedberg, R. 2006. "The Cultural Entrepreneur and the Creative Industries: Beginning in Vienna." *Journal of Cultural Economics* 30, no. 4, pp. 243–61.

Tavin, K. March, 2001. "The Impact of Visual Culture on Art Education." *Panel Presentation at the National Art Education Association Convention.* New York, NY.

Thom, M. 2017. "Arts Entrepreneurship Education in the UK and Germany." *Education + Training* 59, no. 4, pp. 406–26.

Vesper, K. 1992. "New-Venture Ideas: Do Not Overlook the Experience Factor." In *The Entrepreneurial Venture,* eds. W. Sahlman and H. Stevenson, 73–80. Boston, MA: Harvard Business School Publications.

Wagner-Ott, A. 2002. "Analysis of Gender Identity Through Doll and Action Figure Politics in Art Education." *Studies in Art Education* 43, no. 3, pp. 246–63.

Wallace, W. 1994. *Michelangelo at San Lorenzo—Genius as an Entrepreneur.* Cambridge University Press.

Webb, D. 2014. "Placemaking and Social Equity: Expanding the Framework of Creative Placemaking." *Artivate: A Journal of Entrepreneurship in the Arts* 3, no. 1. pp. 35–48.

Welsh, D.H.B., T. Onishi, R.H. DeHoog, S. Syed. 2014. "Responding to the Needs and Challenges of Arts Entrepreneurs: An Exploratory Study of Arts Entrepreneurship in North Caroling Higher Education." *Artivate: A Journal of Entrepreneurship in the Arts* 3, no. 2, pp. 21–37.

White, J. 2013. "Barriers to Recognizing Arts Entrepreneurship Education As Essential to Professional Arts Training." *Artivate: A Journal of Entrepreneurship in the Arts* 2, no. 3, pp. 28–39.

Wilson, B. March, 2001. *Panel Presentation on Visual Culture at the National Art Education Association.* Convention, New York, NY.

CHAPTER 10

Strategic Thinking in Arts Entrepreneurship

Todd A. Stuart

Alice—Which way should I go?
Cat—That depends on where you are going.
Alice—I don't know where I'm going!
Cat—Then it doesn't matter which way you go!

—Lewis Carroll

Sometimes, one is not sure which way to go; they go for the experience. The journey is a divergent creative exploration. Then sometimes, the journey requires an understanding of where they are, where they are going, and the best way to get there. They need to understand the context and then converge on a course of action. Strategic thinking can bridge divergent and convergent journeys and for the arts entrepreneur these thinking skills are identified as both "essential" (Pollard and Wilson 2013, p. 3) and "crucial" (Thom 2016, p. 3). Strategic thinking can be utilized at the intersection of art and entrepreneurship to explore strategies for how the arts can solve both well-defined technical challenges and more importantly messy, adaptive challenges (Ertel and Soloman 2014). In order to apply strategic thinking to the arts entrepreneur's practice, it is important to understand what arts entrepreneurship is, the context in which arts entrepreneurs operate, and the differences between strategy, strategic planning and strategic thinking. Then, the journey can begin.

Arts Entrepreneurship?

Human nature insists on a definition for every concept.
—Henry Mintzberg

The field of arts entrepreneurship is still developing as an area of academic study and as an arts practice. Questions about the field are discussed and debated. The definition of what exactly arts entrepreneurship is has not yet been settled and their role in society is not agreed upon. Gary D. Beckman (Beckman, 2014, p. 10) states that "If there were ever two words brought together to form an emerging academic field wrought with little to no consensus on what each word means, ART + ENTREPRENEURSHIP would be a strong candidate." So, while ten people might have ten different interpretations, a starting point is important in order to discuss how other concepts connect to arts entrepreneurship. Beckman goes on to offer a starting point for this initial interpretation, "while we can define 'Arts Entrepreneurship' using extant definitions, we must ask whether or not a precise definition is even possible in the future..." (Beckman 2014, p. 10). Maybe, a "precise definition" is not needed at this point. Thinking how a sculptor might approach a block of marble, first roughing out a figure and then later honing the work to give it more definition and detail. Other "wrought" fields have the same challenge, in the field of strategy Henry Mintzberg points out "explicit recognition of multiple definitions can help practitioners and researchers alike to maneuver through this difficult field." So for now at least, a Design Thinking prototype made from "extant" definitions is a start. Table 10.1 lists these definitions to use for this prototype.

A synthesis of these three definitions yields the following:

"Using creativity and imagination, the Arts Entrepreneur creates works of beauty and emotional power that are about fostering an ingenious human spirit to improve humankind and change the world" (Oxford Dictionary Online; Timmons; Neck 2014).

This prototype provides a starting point to discuss how strategic thinking can be utilized in arts entrepreneurship.

Table 10.1 Extant definitions of Art and Entrepreneurship

Definition	Source
Art is "The expression or application of human creative skill and imagination, typically in a visual form such as painting or sculpture, producing works to be appreciated primarily for their beauty or emotional power."	Oxford Dictionary Online
"Entrepreneurship will create a better world. It's not just about new company, capital and job formation, nor innovation, nor creativity, nor breakthroughs. It is also about fostering an ingenious human spirit and improving humankind."	Jeffry A. Timmons
Entrepreneurship is "A way of thinking and acting that can change the world"	Heidi Neck

(Oxford Dictionary Online; Timmons; Neck 2014)

Context of the Arts Entrepreneur?

Hey, it's crazy out there!

—Nathan Bennett and G. James Lemoine

Arts entrepreneurs are creating works in an increasingly challenging world. The world today has been described as a "VUCA world" characterized as a world of volatility, uncertainty, complexity and ambiguity," (Bennett and Lemoine 2014, p. 311). A "VUCA world" is not necessarily new for artists. From the earliest cave painters to street artists today the world was and is volatile, uncertain, ambiguous and complex though growing more complex with many new challenges. Technology has democratized artistic production and the audiences are moving from passive consumption to active participation changing the artist/audience dynamic (Cameron 2010). Artist and arts organizations are working to become re-engaged with their communities. Communities where demographics are changing, funding models are evolving and people are questioning the values of the arts. In a world where the only constant is change, having a strategic position is critical yet some have questioned the validity of strategy. Kevin Roberts, the former CEO of Saatchi and Saatchi, said—"I am sick of strategy." He also reportedly claimed that strategy is dead; a quick Google search will show that many others have made the same claim. Strategic plans, required by some grantors in the arts, are seen as antithetical to the field, and some arts professionals argue that corporate strategic planning focused on profits while their job was to focus on the art and not the profit (Kaiser, Engler, and Lucey 1995). To complicate the situation even further, strategy, strategic planning, and strategic thinking are sometimes used interchangeably even though they are different concepts. Understanding the differences between the concepts will help the arts entrepreneurs to best utilize strategic thinking in their practice.

Strategy, Strategic Planning and Strategic Thinking

Strategy is "an organized pattern of behavior toward an end."
—David La Piana

The concept of strategy has roots in military usage in both Eastern and Western Cultures. In the East, military strategies were detailed in The Art of War by Sun Tzu "the most complete and reputable book on military strategy that has survived to date," (Chen 1994, p. 42). In the West, Bracker (1980) pointed out that strategy was derived from the Greek word *strategos* which means "a general" and that strategy was not limited to the military; it was also discussed by artists of the time such as Homer and Euripides. In the 20th century, influential business thinkers like Peter Drucker and Michael Porter championed strategy and strategic planning. In *How Competitive Forces Shape Strategy*, Michael Porter supports an analytical approach to creating strategies and argued, "The essence of strategy formulation is coping with competition," (Porter 1979, p. 102). Strategic planning was the analytical planning process used to develop strategies. Strategies were then broken into tactics that managers implemented with the purpose of gaining market share and beating the competition. Figure 10.1 illustrates the traditional Strategic Planning process.

Strategic planning ———→ Strategies ———→ Implementation

Figure 10.1 Traditional strategic planning process

The problem with traditional strategic planning as Henry Mintzberg points out is that "the world is supposed to hold still while a plan is being developed and then stay on the predicted course while that plan is being implemented" (Mintzberg 1994, p. 112).

Accepting this line of thought creates a tension between the unpredictability of the future and the need for strategies. Breaking the traditional planning process into the components of developing strategies and implementing strategies allows for the thinking and the doing to be separated. This is illustrated in Figure 10.2.

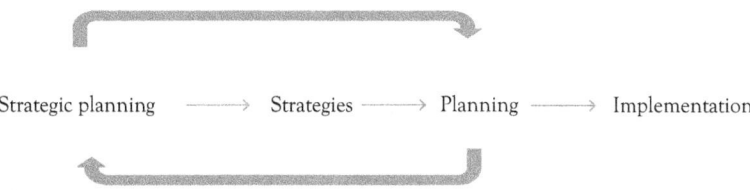

Strategic planning ⟶ Strategies ⟶ Planning ⟶ Implementation

Figure 10.2 Strategic thinking process

In this model the purpose of the planning is to put the strategies developed during the strategic thinking process into action (Heracleous 1998). Strategic thinking is then the creative process utilized in developing actionable strategies.

There are many perspectives to consider in understanding strategic thinking. Henry Mintzberg (1994) describes strategic thinking as a synthesis of intuition and creativity leading to a vision of the future though the vision is not fully formed. Zahra and Nambisan (2012, p. 220) points out "strategic thinking focuses on visualizing the future before it happens a process that entails building and considering different scenarios." Table 10.2 illustrated these and other perspectives on strategic thinking.

This common thread of vision and creativity in the prototype of arts entrepreneurship discussed earlier in the chapter and is central to all the perspectives on strategic thinking.

Table 10.2 Perspectives on strategic thinking

Mintzberg	Zahra and Nambisan	Bonn	Leidtka	Abraham
Synthesis	Requirements	Elements	Attributes	Approaches
Imagination	Creativity	Creativity	Intelligently opportunistic	Finding new opportunities
Creativity	Foresight	Vision	Thinking in time	Being future-oriented
Vision	Insight	Systems thinking	A systems or holistic view	Being collaborative
			A focus on intent	Being successfully different
			Hypothesis-driven	Emulating entrepreneurs

(Mintzberg 1994; Bonn 2005; Zahra and Nambisan 2012; Leidtka 1998; Abraham 2005)

Strategic Thinking and the Arts Entrepreneur

.... The explorer leads from the front not by issuing directions, but by asking strategically purposeful questions.

—Tim Brown

Questions are important in art and arts entrepreneurship. The ability to ask good questions can be more important than the answers (Brown 2016). Questions start the creative process of discovery, discovery of good problems to solve. Not existing problems, but problems that have not before been poised (Getzels and Csikszentmihalyi 1966). For the arts entrepreneur, these problems can be addressed through the entrepreneurial-strategic-managerial thinking process.

In *What makes entrepreneurs entrepreneurial?* Professor Saras D. Sarasvathy (2001) describes different modes of thinking and reasoning that differentiates the approach that managers take from the approach that entrepreneurs take. In managerial thinking, there is a goal that is pre-determined, and the job is to take existing resources, or "means," and find the most efficient way to achieve the goal. In entrepreneurial thinking, the entrepreneur takes the same "means" but is not limited to the pre-determined goal. The entrepreneur takes the "means" and imagines new goals or "imagine ends" that do not currently exist. The entrepreneurial thinker diverges on the given set of means while the managerial thinker uses the means to converge on a pre-determined goal. The entrepreneur finds new problems to solve with existing "means." Both methods of thinking are important for the entrepreneur as Sarasvathy (2001, p. 2) points out "the best entrepreneurs are capable of both and do use both modes very well." Sarasvathy differentiates strategic thinkers as creators of new ways to get to the same predetermined goals that the managerial thinker is seeking (Sarasvathy 2001). This viewpoint illustrates the inherent creativity of the strategic thinking but does not link it to the entrepreneurial thinking process. By making this link, strategic thinking can serve as an integrated bridge between entrepreneurial and managerial thinking. A model of strategic thinking as a bridge is illustrated in Figure 10.3.

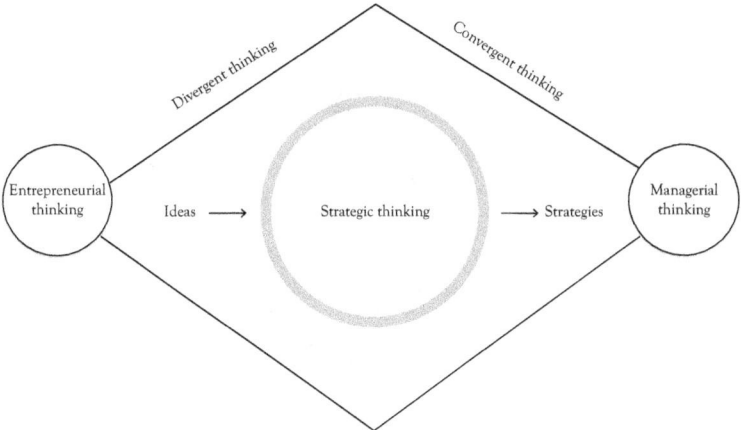

Figure 10.3 Strategic thinking bridge

In this model, strategic thinking is both a divergent and convergent activity. The strategic thinker uses ideas developed in the entrepreneurial thinking process and converts them into actionable strategies that can be operationalized in the managerial thinking process.

When developing strategies in this iterative process, arts entrepreneurs can utilize design, systems and integrative thinking to fully explore ideas developed in the entrepreneurial process. Design thinking can be thought of as a system of innovation with overlapping spaces of inspiration, ideation and implementation (Brown 2009). Strategic thinkers explore insights developed in this user-centered method to prototype and test strategies. During this process they need to adopt the "Art" of integrative thinking and "embrace complexity, tolerate uncertainty, and manage tension in searching for creative solutions to problems," (Martin and Austen 1999, p. 2). Also, these problems need to be put in the broader systems thinking context to understand how the parts influence and connect to the whole (Ackoff, Ackoff and Emery 2005). These modes of thinking are utilized in the strategic thinking process and guided by the vision or the purpose of the arts entrepreneur's exploration. Figure 10.4 demonstrates this relationship.

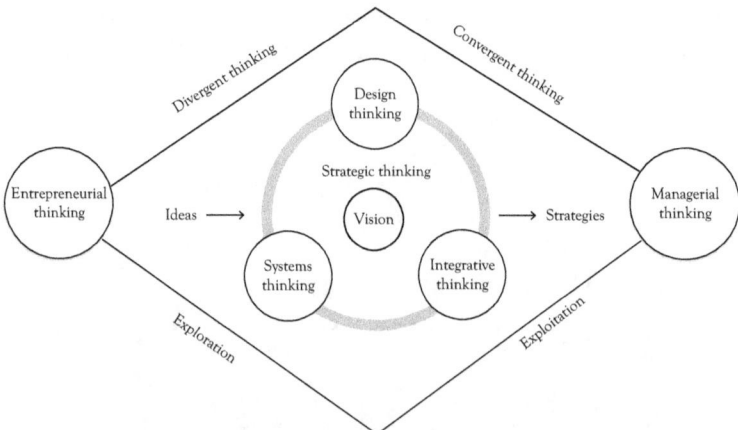

Figure 10.4 Strategic thinking bridge with modes of thinking

Ideas are the inputs to strategic thinking and strategies are the outputs. Another way to think about this is that strategic thinking is the intersection of the explorative nature of entrepreneurial thinking and the exploitive nature of managerial thinking. March (1991, p. 7) gives insight to these concepts: "Exploration includes things captured by terms such as search, variation, risk taking, experimentation, play, flexibility, discovery, innovation. Exploitation includes such things as refinement, choice, production, efficiency, selection, implementation, execution." With this model in mind, the following fictitious example illustrates how the arts entrepreneur can utilize strategic thinking. Mary is an arts entrepreneur in a medium sized city. She is already an entrepreneurial thinker who knows her means: who she is, what she knows, and who she knows. She also knows who she might be able to enlist in her journey and what resources she is willing to risk—her affordable loss (Sarasvathy 2001). Mary has a background in studio art and has a vision of making artist's lives better by creating market opportunities (income) for them. In her community, she has noticed the prevalence of unknown artists that do not have an outlet to display and sell their work in the formal gallery environment. She also has noticed that most of her peers, just starting their careers, do not own much art. She wonders if there is an opportunity for connecting these two groups. Utilizing her design thinking skills, she starts to interview both the artists and her peers who she thinks might be interested in the artist's work. She is looking for an insight that will help connect the artists and potential buyers. She also is using a systems thinking perspective to understand how art is currently acquired and sold in her city and how creating this connection might benefit the community as a whole. She has spoken with city officials about using an old, underutilized gym that the city owns as a possible community gallery. As an artist, Mary has dealt with ambiguity in her own work and career. It is difficult in today's business driven culture to be an artist and there is a lot of uncertainly in her life. While she is not aware of it she has become very good, like many artists, at integrative thinking.

Mary knows that the best way to test her theory of a mutually beneficial community art gallery is to prototype it. On a Saturday in June, she sets up a tent in front of the old gym, and for three hours the ten artists that she recruited show their work. Through her marketing efforts, forty people show up and three small pieces of art are sold. She interviews the artists and community members about the current art system and the potential for a community gallery. Mary thinks the test was successful and she finds an interesting and surprising insight. Many of the community members are renters and expect to move within the next couple of years. They are apprehensive of buying some of the larger works of art due to the challenge of moving art and the possibility that the art will not fit in their next residence.

With this new knowledge, she develops a business model where community members rent the works with an option to buy. The artists will have some monthly income and the community members have the ability to either return the art or trade it for another work of art when they relocate. Mary also realizes the need for an art packing and delivery service and includes that in her model. Mary continues to iterate through the different modes of thinking as she synthesizes her strategies to make the community gallery a reality.

Through this strategic thinking process Mary has developed the following strategies for her arts entrepreneurial venture that she believe will help her achieve her vision:

1. Create art rentals that will connect underserved artists and patrons
2. Develop art packing and delivery services to protect and increase art rentals
3. Leverage underutilized city resources to benefit artists and the community

Mary now can take the next step and operationalize her strategies. She has successfully demonstrated her ability to be a strategic thinker.

Moving Forward with Strategic Thinking

Is this process of measurable discovery also involved in the wider range of human creativity…?
                                    —Jacob W. Getzels and Mihaly Csikszentmihalyi

At the intersection of art and entrepreneurship, arts entrepreneurs envision a future that benefits humankind by creating innovative strategies to deploy art in the world to solve problems. The arts entrepreneur utilizes all modes of thinking discussed here in their practice and use strategic thinking specifically to bridge entrepreneurial and managerial thinking and to "… resolve ambiguity and make sense of a complex world," (Bonn 2005, p. 338). This relatively new field of study and practice is still developing into a discipline. Maybe, the next step is to develop a method for arts entrepreneurship to explore. A method infused with both art and entrepreneurship.

"In an ever-changing world, we need to teach methods that stand the test of dramatic changes in content and context. At the end of the day, perhaps we do not teach entrepreneurship the discipline. Perhaps we teach a method to navigate the discipline." (Neck and Greene 2011, p. 68)

As arts entrepreneurs develop a method to their practice, they will continue to ask many strategic questions. What is synthesis of art and entrepreneurship? What does it mean to be an arts entrepreneur? What are the next steps and how will we get there? Questions answered by exploring the experience as they make the journey. So, let the journey begin.

References

Abraham, S. 2005. "Stretching Strategic Thinking." *Strategy & Leadership* 33, no. 5, pp. 5–12.

Ackoff, R.L., R.L. Ackoff, and F.E. Emery. 2005. *On Purposeful Systems: An Interdisciplinary Analysis of Individual and Social Behavior as a System of Purposeful Events.* AldineTransaction.

Beckman, G.D. 2014. "What Arts Entrepreneurship Isn't." *Journal of Arts Entrepreneurship Research* 1, no. 1, pp. 3–17.

Bennett, N., and J. Lemoine. 2014. "What VUCA Really Means for You." *Harvard Business Review*, January-February 27.

Bonn, I. 2001. "Developing Strategic Thinking as a Core Competency." *Management Decision* 39, no. 1, pp. 63–71.

Bonn, I. 2005. "Improving Strategic Thinking: A Multilevel Approach." *Leadership & Organization Development Journal* 26, no. 5, pp. 336–54.

Brown, T. 2009. *Change by Design: How Design Thinking Transforms Organizations and Inspires Innovation.* New York: Harper Collins.

Brown, T. 2016. "Leaders Can Turn Creativity into a Competitive Advantage" HBR.org, November 2, 2016. https://hbr.org/2016/11/leaders-can-turn-creativity-into-a-competitive-advantage

Cameron, B. 2010. "Why the Live Arts Matter." TedTalk video, 12:37. Posted September 2010. https://ted.com/talks/ben_cameron_tedxyyc

Carroll, L. 1917. *Through the Looking Glass: And What Alice Found There.* Rand, McNally.

Chen, M. 1994. "Sun Tzu's Strategic Thinking and Contemporary Business." *Business Horizons* 37, no. 2, pp. 42–48.

Ertel, C., and L.K. Solomon. 2014. *Moments of Impact: How to Design Strategic Conversations that Accelerate Change.* New York: Simon and Schuster.

Getzels, J.W., and M. Csikszentmihalyi. 1966. "Portrait of the Artist as an Explorer." *Transaction* 3, no. 6, pp. 31–34.

Henderson, B.D. 1989. "The Origin of Strategy." *Harvard Business Review* 67, no. 6, pp. 139–43.

Heracleous, L. 1998: "Strategic Thinking or Strategic Planning?" *Long Range Planning* 31, no. 3, pp. 481–87.

Kaiser, M.M., P.S. Engler, and P. Lucey. 1995. *Strategic Planning in the Arts: A Practical Guide.* Kaiser/Engler Group.

La Piana, D. 2008. *The Nonprofit Strategy Revolution: Real-Time Strategic Planning in a Rapid-Response World.* Fieldstone Alliance.

Liedtka, J.M. 1998. "Strategic Thinking: Can it be Taught?." *Long Range Planning* 31, no. 1, pp. 120–29.

March, J.G. 1991. "Exploration and Exploitation in Organizational Learning." *Organization Science* 2, no. 1, pp. 71–87.

Martin, R., and H. Austen. 1999. "The Art of Integrative Thinking." *Rotman Management*, pp. 2–5.

Mintzberg, H. 1994. "The Fall and Rise of Strategic Planning." *Harvard Business Review* 72, no. 1, pp. 107–14.

Mintzberg, H. 1997. "The Strategy Concept I: Five Ps for Strategy." *California Management Review* 30, no. 1, pp. 11–24.

Nasi, J (Ed.). 1991. *Arenas of Strategic Thinking*, 29. Foundation for Economic Education, Helsinki, Finland.

Neck, H. 2014. "Teaching Entrepreneurship: A Practice-Based Approach— Interview with Co-author." YouTube video, 2:00. Posted December 12, 2014. https://youtube.com/watch?v=PpZKT8crLK0&t=6s

Neck, H., and P. Greene. 2011. "Entrepreneurship Education: Known Worlds and New Frontiers." *Journal of Small Business Management* 49, no. 1, pp. 55–70.

Oxford Dictionary Online. 2014. "art," accessed June 5, 2017. https://en.oxforddictionaries.com/definition/art

Pollard, V., and E. Wilson. 2013. "The 'Entrepreneurial Mindset' in Creative and Performing Arts Higher Education in Australia." *Artivate: A Journal of Entrepreneurship in the Arts* 3, no. 1, pp. 3–22.

Porter, M.E. 1979. "Competitive Forces Shape Strategy." *Harvard Business Review*, pp. 137–45.

Roberts, K. 2015. "DMA Keynote Kevin Roberts" YouTube video, 48.58:25. Posted October 23, 2015. https://youtube.com/watch?v=ZTYisjudhk

Sarasvathy, S.D. 2001. "What Makes Entrepreneurs Entrepreneurial?" submitted to *Harvard Business Review*.

Thom, M. 2016. "Crucial Skills for the Entrepreneurial Success of Fine Artists." *Artivate: A Journal of Entrepreneurship in the Arts* 5, no. 1, pp. 3–24.

Timmons, J.A. July 2014. *quoted in Price-Babson SEE Brochure.* Babson College.

Zahra, S.A., and S. Nambisan. 2012. "Entrepreneurship and Strategic Thinking in Business Ecosystems." *Business Horizons* 55, no. 3, pp. 219–29.

Conclusion

J. Mark Munoz and Julienne W. Shields

Arts entrepreneurship is an emerging and growing area in business that has attracted artists, creatives, and practitioners from all over the world. In the United States, there are over 700,000 businesses pertaining to art creation and distribution creating approximately 2.9 million jobs (Americansforthearts.org 2016). It is a field that covers a broad range of the artistic endeavors, and is implemented in diverse ways.

The chapters in this book indicate that arts entrepreneurship impacts life and business in profound ways. The chapters in the book expanded understanding of arts entrepreneurship, linked its implications on culture, values, and internationalization, and offered pathways—including tools and knowledge—to support the growth and success of arts enterprises.

Based on the chapter contents, academic research and professional experience, the authors identified ten (10) key strategies that are important to the practice of arts entrepreneurship. These strategies are highlighted in Table C.1.

Table C.1 Key strategies in arts entrepreneurship

Balance	Success in the practice of arts entrepreneurship requires finding the balance between artistic and business demands.
Timing	Execution of courses of action needs to be at a proper time that is suitable to customer and market needs, policies and competitive pressures.
Value	Art is valued in different criteria. It is important for artist entrepreneurs to fully understand their value proposition and build on areas where they can best connect with consumers who will most appreciate their vision and voice to optimize profitability.
Knowledge	A keen understanding of the operational environment is important. Artist entrepreneurs need to be aware of trends, customer expectations, competitive terrain, and even the usage of technology to accelerate their business.

Depth	A shallow understanding of business concepts is not enough for an artist to be commercially successful. Deep knowledge of concepts relating to marketing, financial matters, networks, and effective management is important.
Socialization	Networking and relationship building is critical for arts enterprises. Development of a strong rapport with various stakeholders will have aid the artistic enterprise.
Technology	Several arts ventures have leveraged technology effectively to boost sales and improve business efficiency. Investment in technology and carefully planning its utilization in the enterprise can yield positive results.
Adaptability	The very nature of art is grounded on change and evolution. Consumer tastes and preferences change, policies that support the arts fluctuate, and social and technological climates shift. Therefore arts enterprises need to be able to change quickly with the times.
Partnering	Some arts enterprises have grown their business by working with the right strategic partner. Finding like-minded firms where synergies can be built can be beneficial.
Growth	Artists entrepreneurs need to make a serious effort to grow. Given the competitive and evolving nature of the business, planning for and pursuing a definitive pathway toward self-betterment is essential.

In order to assist the reader in thinking about specific approaches to implement arts entrepreneurship strategies, a Strategic Assessment Guide is provided in Table C.2. In this table, selected questions are offered to help the reader think through the key issues.

Table C.2 Strategic assessment guide

Balance	What are my current artistic interests and demands? What are pressing business needs? What are priorities? What do I need to do to find the right balance? What resources will I need to make this happen?
Timing	What are the current needs of my customers? What are the current demands of the market? In what ways are my competitors superior to me? What are current policies and programs available that I can utilize? How do I respond to customer and market needs and competitive pressures in a timely manner? What do I need to make this happen? When do I make this happen?
Value	What is the value proposition of my business? Do my employees, partners, customers and other stakeholders know this? Does my value proposition translate to profitability? Why or why not? What needs to change? What do I need to make the changes?

Knowledge	Do I thoroughly understand my operating business environment? What are the current trends? What are customer expectations? How is the political and economic environment influencing the arts industry? How is technology changing my business? How are trends and customers changing my business? What does the competitive terrain look like? Who are my toughest competitors and why?
Depth	How well do I know business concepts (i.e., marketing, accounting, finance, management)? With which aspects of business am I strong? Where am I weak? What changes need to take place? What areas do I need to learn more about? What skill sets do I need to hire in my organization? What would it take to make this happen? What would it cost to make this happen? When does this need to happen?
Socialization	On a scale of 1–10, how would I rate my networking ability (1-lowest, 10 highest)? Why? Is this adequate for the business? On a scale of 1-10, how would I rate my relationship building ability (1-lowest, 10 highest)? Why? How has this impacted my business? How would I rate my organization in both areas? What needs to change and how? What would it take? What is my relationship like with other stakeholders (i.e., community, board, investors)? How can this be improved?
Technology	On a scale of 1-10, how effective is technology in my business (1-lowest, 10-highest)? Why? What can be done better? What resources do I need to optimize performance?
Adaptability	On a scale of 1-10, how adaptable is my organization (1-lowest, 10-highest)? Why? What changes need to happen? How can these changes be made and by when? What changes or shifts in policy can be anticipated? How can those be mitigated should they come to pass? Should I restructure my organization? How?
Partnering	What types of other ventures or firms might offer synergy with my business? Would partnering with them provide unique opportunities to strengthen my value proposition? compete better? improve profitability or financial self-sufficiency? How can these partnerships be structured? What are the cost and resource implications?
Growth	With regard to personal development, which areas need the most attention? Where do I need to grow? How do I execute these growth plans? How much would it cost? When does this need to happen and why? What are the strengths, weaknesses, opportunities, and threats relating to my enterprise? Considering these, what changes can I make that would have the most significant impact on my business and profitability? Which of these should be priorities? Where does the organization need grow?

Identification of specific tasks can be helpful in plotting an effective action agenda. Table C.3 highlights a Strategic Action Plan for art entrepreneurs.

Table C.3 Strategic action plan for artist entrepreneurs

Strategy Action Steps

Strategy	Action Steps
Balance	(1) Assess current artistic interests. (2) Assess current business needs. (3) List and evaluate priorities. (4) Create a plan of action. (5) Identify timeline and resources needed to implement plan. (6) Implement plan. (7) Review, evaluate and revise plan as needed.
Timing	(1) Evaluate current interests, passions, curiosities. (2) Conduct research and identify needs and patterns of customers. (3) Conduct research and identify needs of market. (4) Conduct competition research and analysis. (5) Develop a plan of action based on the nexus of self-reflection and findings of customers, market, and competition. (6) Identify resources needed and timing of implementation. (7) Implement plan with consideration placed on timing and impact. (8) Review, evaluate and revise plan as needed.
Value	(1) Arrange a series organizational meetings directed at identifying the value proposition of the artistic venture. (2) Validate meeting discussions with research. (3) Designate a team to examine and evaluate the financial implications of your company's value proposition. (4) Develop a plan of action to optimize value proposition with regards to the appropriate customer segments. (5) Implement plan with priority placed on its impact on profitability. (6) Review, evaluate and revise plan as needed based on business results.
Knowledge	(1) Utilize an internal or external advisory team to conduct research on your industry (i.e., trends, customer expectations, competition, technology). (2) Design strategies for customer discovery (understanding the needs, desires, and goals of customers, clients, audiences, etc.). (3) Discuss findings with the management or advisory team and assess business impact. (4) Develop a plan of action to translate gained knowledge to improvement. (5) Implement a plan of action to optimize knowledge gathering and analysis. (6) Review, evaluate and revise plan as needed.
Depth	(1) Assess your personal competencies in business (i.e., marketing, accounting, finance, and management). Identify your strengths and weaknesses. (2) Assess your advisory team's competencies in business (i.e., marketing, accounting, finance, and management). Identify strengths and weaknesses.

	(3) Evaluate your venture's overall business competence within its artistic context.
	(4) Develop a plan of action that builds on strengths and addresses weaknesses. The creation of a Skills Development Plan and/or a talent or partner acquisition plan would be helpful.
	(5) Implement the plan noting when a pivot is needed.
	(6) Review, evaluate and revise plan as needed.
Socialization	(1) Assess your personal networking and relationship building ability.
	(2) Assess your venture's networking and relationship building ability.
	(3) Evaluate strengths and weaknesses.
	(4) Develop a plan for improvement.
	(5) Implement the plan noting when pivoting is necessary.
	(6) Review, evaluate and revise plan as needed.
Technology	(1) Assess your personal technology competencies.
	(2) Assess available technology competencies and channels in use by customers and partners.
	(3) Evaluate strengths and weaknesses.
	(4) Develop a plan for improvement considering resources needed and timing.
	(5) Implement the plan noting when pivoting is necessary.
	(6) Review, evaluate and revise plan as needed.
Adaptability	(1) Assess your venture's level of adaptability.
	(2) Examine performance of competitors.
	(3) Identify best practices of industry stars.
	(4) Identify areas where changes can be made in your business.
	(5) Develop a plan of action considering resources needed and timing.
	(6) Implement the plan noting when pivoting is necessary.
	(7) Review, evaluate and revise plan as needed.
Partnering	(1) Identify areas in your business that can benefit from strategic partnering.
	(2) Create a list of potential partners and evaluate derived advantages.
	(3) Identify a short list of the best potential partners.
	(4) Develop a strategic partnership plan including viable structures, resources needed, and timing of implementation.
	(5) Implement the plan noting when pivoting is necessary.
	(6) Review, evaluate and revise plan as needed.
Growth	(1) Conduct a SWOT analysis of your enterprise.
	(2) Conduct a SWOT analysis of your industry including policies that impact that industry.
	(3) Identify changes that need to be made to best respond to competitive threats and capture emerging opportunities.
	1. Prioritize planned changes.
	2. Create an Growth Plan considering personal and organizational needs.
	3. Weigh in cost and resource considerations as well as timing.
	4. Create a series of small market tests you can do for minimal cost that can inform your Growth Plan.

	5. Use results obtained with the small market tests to either support or refute the assumptions on which you built your plan.
	6. Revise and implement the plan to scale. Pivoting may be minimal if you have done a thorough job of creating market tests that are particularly relevant.
	7. Review, evaluate and revise plan as needed.

Table C.3 outlines suggested action steps that can be taken to implement strategic changes for arts enterprises. This serves as a blueprint for business enhancement. Since organizations vary, this approach should not be viewed as a one size fits all model. Its implementation can be tailored to best suit an organization's goals, resources, and priorities.

The pathway to successful arts enterprises is not an easy path. There are countless factors to consider and evaluate. Organizations will be well served by keeping an open attitude and constantly seeking ways to improve. After all, creative industries set the stage for innovation and development (Bilton 2007). This is referred in the preceding table as pivoting, and it is important to stay nimble in competitive industries.

There is a high need to differentiate. Some artist entrepreneurs established creative social enterprises to become unique, heighten value proposition, and enhance community engagement. Trapp (2015) highlights the case of Earthen Symphony a decorative art studio in India focused on training and providing jobs for designers and artisans. Success in the industry requires a strong ability to gather and analyze information. Microenterprises in the craft industry need to develop a strong marketing strategy (Kean, Niemeyer, and Miller 1996). Communication skills and financial acumen are important skill considerations. Entrepreneurship and leadership plays an important role in the arts (Henry 2007; Lapierre 2001).

In addition to the aforementioned, the authors recommend considering the following:

Professional memberships—being a part of a professional organization in the arts or business can help expand knowledge on the practice. For example, an organization such as the Society for Arts Entrepreneurship Education offers several developmental and networking opportunities. Association of Arts Administration Educators also has arts entrepreneurship within its various focal areas, and the United States Association of Small Business and Entrepreneurship has a dynamic special interest group called Creative and Arts Entrepreneurship.

Mentors—find a suitable mentor for business or the chosen craft. There are opportunities for finding mentors in business, academe, arts, and the non-profit sectors. Mentors can be invited to be a part of your organization as Advisory Board members.

Personal development—attending conferences and workshops on arts entrepreneurship can help one grow and be up to date with emerging trends. Taking formal arts and business classes can be helpful. Several arts and entrepreneurship academic programs are being created worldwide. There is an annual Self-employment in the Arts (SEA) conference for artists of any discipline to share best practices and gain inspiration.

Social networks—being part of an art community online and offline and can expand ones network. In addition, sharing work spaces or being part of a start-up incubator or accelerator can help one find useful support.

Art communities—creating or being a part of art communities can offer value. The authors recommend the formation of Art Economic Zones (AEZ) where art business can be housed together under one roof and gain cost efficiencies and economies of scale. This model may also lead to negotiated tax breaks from the local government. In addition to cost benefits, AEZ's can also offer ease of access to technology, marketing and internationalization expertise, project funding, and training and development. The authors are exploring the possibility of piloting an AEZ based on the Microenterprise Economic Zone (MEZO) model originally introduced by J. Mark Munoz (2010) in the book "Contemporary Microenterprise."

As more arts enterprises flourish, exciting business models will emerge. Keeping an eye on the best practices in the field would be helpful. For example, Social Print Studio, a California printing company that preserves Instagram memories for clients was ranked 66 among the Inc 5000 fastest growing companies in America with a sales increase of 4,100 percent (Godfrey 2016). Ultimately, learning and applying effective business practices will optimize the potential of arts enterprises.

References

Americansforthearts.org. 2016. Business and Employment in the Arts: Measuring the Scope of the Nation's Art-Related Industries. Viewable at http://americansforthearts.org/by-program/reports-and-data/research-studies-publications/creative-industries (accessed October 7, 2016).

Bilton, C. 2007. *Management and Creativity*. Oxford: Blackwell.

Godfrey, E. 2016. "How Performance Art Turned into one of America's Fastest Growing Businesses." Accessed at Inc.com on October 7, 2016. Viewable at http://inc.com/elaine-godfrey/2015-inc5000-performance-art-piece-into-a-successful-photo-printing-studio.html

Henry, C. 2007. *Entrepreneurship in the Creative Industries: An International Perspective*. Cheltenham: Edward Elgar.

Kean, R.C., S. Niemeyer, and N.J. Miller. 1996. "Competitive Strategies in the Craft Product Retailing Industry." *Journal of Small Business Management* 34, no. 1, pp. 13–23.

Lapierre, L. 2001. "Leadership and Arts Management." *International Journal of Arts Management* 3, no. 3, pp. 4–12.

Munoz, J.M. 2010. *Contemporary Microenterprise: Concepts and Cases*. London: Edward Elgar Publishing.

Trapp, R. 2015. "The Creative Social Enterprise: An Impact Investment." GIA Reader. Viewable at http://giarts.org/article/creative-social-enterprise-impact-investment (accessed October 14, 2016).

About the Contributors

Dr Melissa Crum is an artist, author, researcher, and founder of Mosaic Education Network, LLC. Mosaic Education Network is a consulting company that infuses the arts, research, storytelling and critical thinking into professional development, community building, and curriculum development. Mosaic helps participants have healthy ways of thinking about themselves, their future, and their connection to a diverse world. She has conducted professional development trainings, given presentations, and facilitated projects across the United States and internationally. Dr Crum also uses her skills to fulfill her role as an ARTrepreneur Specialist working with the Barnett Center for Integrated Arts and Enterprise at The Ohio State University. Through her position, she aides in creating a skills-sharing community of novices and new business owners and experts.

Dr Per Darmer is an associate professor at Copenhagen Business School (CBS) and a member of imagine center for creative industries research. He has coedited "Creating Experiences in the Experience Economy," Elward Elgar (2008), and managed a number of major research projects such as "Cinema" (2004 to 2007). His area of interest is organizational theory and the Danish music and film industries, as well as the relationship between art and organizing are among the contexts of his studies.

Andreja Jaklic is a full professor and research fellow at the Centre of International Relations at the Faculty of Social Sciences, University of Ljubljana in Slovenia. Her research and teaching spans across three disciplinary areas, including International Business, International Economics, and European studies (EU in a global economy). Her main research interests are on internationalization, export, foreign direct investment, foreign entry strategy, multinational enterprises, particularly multinational enterprises from former transition economies and their effects on competitiveness, growth, productivity, and innovation. She earned her experience from several academic and applied international research projects (European framework programs, COST Action program and regional projects, business intelligence projects and workshops, consultancy to international organizations (such as European commission, UNCTAD and the OECD), as well as to national governmental agencies and business. Her publications include monographs, *Enhanced Transition through Outward Internationalization: Outward FDI by Slovenian Firms* (Ashgate Publishing 2003), several book chapters and over 30 articles, also in *Journal of World Business, Transnational Corporations, The Services Industries Journal, Eastern European Economies and Post-Communist Economies*. She is a co-founder and executive board member of Academy of International Business Central and Easter European Chapter (AIB—CEEC) and served as board member of European Academy of International Business (EIBA) from 2010 to 2016.

Paraskevi Karageorgu is a graduate in European studies. He specialized in European Cultural Policies (MA thesis research at KU Leuven) and has working experience from Ljubljana International Film Festival. He collaborated as journalist with Cineuropa—media for European Cinema and was a Jury Member of the Venice Days 2016.

Dr Sonia BasSheva Mañjon is the inaugural director of the Lawrence and Isabel Barnett Center for Integrated Arts and Enterprise, Associate Professor of Arts Administration, Education and Policy, Affiliate Faculty in Latina/o Studies and The STEAM Factory at The Ohio State University. The Center's mission is to educate and prepare students for successful careers in the arts and related entrepreneurial fields through advancing and increasing an understanding of the business side of the arts and the worlds of arts management, policy, and culture. She has more than 25 years of experience in higher education, nonprofit, and government administration. Dr Mañjon is the former executive director of the Center for Art and Public Life, founding chair of the Community Arts major, and held the Simpson Endowed Professorship of Community Arts at the California College of the Arts (CCA). Highlights of her tenure at CCA include executive leadership of a six-year campus-wide diversity initiative, and the establishment of the Community Arts Program, the first BFA program of its kind in the United States. She also created the Center's Visiting Artists and Scholars program; raised over $8 million dollars for CCA initiatives; and implemented 100 Families Oakland: Art & Social Change, a highly successful community program that engaged over 500 Oakland residents in art making and civic engagement. Dr Mañjon publications and video documentaries include: *100 Families Oakland: Art and Social Change; Crafting a Vision for Art, Equity and Civic Engagement: Convening the Community Arts Field in Higher Education; A Snap Shot: Landmarking Community Cultural Arts Organizations Nationally; Invisible Identity: Mujeres Dominicanas en California*; and *Pieces of Cloth, Pieces of Culture: Tapa from Tonga and the Pacific Islands.*

Deirdre McQuillan is a lecturer in strategy and international business at the University of Bradford School of Management. Her research area is grounded in the field of creative professional service firms such as architecture firms. She has published in the Journal of Business Strategy and Advances in Strategic Management on the internationalization process, business modeling, and strategy and talent alignment of creative professional service firms stemming from data collected within the architecture industry.

Robert Moussetis, DBA, has been at North Central College since 1998. He has a passion for international business and has traveled with more than 600 students to more than 20 countries. He has delivered seminars in Abu Dhabi, China, Costa Rica, Greece, and Japan and has presented papers in Austria, Brazil, Greece, Malaysia and Mexico. He has earned four best paper awards and has published articles in journals such as "Competitiveness Review," "Journal of Management History," and "Journal of International Business Research and Practice." He also had eight years of managerial experience at a Fortune 500 firm.

J. Mark Munoz is a tenured Full Professor of International Business at Millikin University in Illinois, and a former Visiting Fellow at the Kennedy School of Government at Harvard University. He is a recipient of several awards including four Best Research Paper Awards, a Literary Award, an International Book Award, and the ACBSP Teaching Excellence Award among others. He was recognized by the Academy of Global Business Advancement as the 2016 Distinguished Business Dean. Aside from top-tier journal publications, he has authored/edited/co-edited 14 books : *Land of My Birth, Winning Across Borders, In Transition, A Salesman in Asia, Handbook of Business Plan Creation, International Social Entrepreneurship, Contemporary Microenterprises : Concepts and Cases, Handbook on the Geopolitics of Business, Hispanic-Latino Entrepreneurship, Business Plan Essentials, Managerial Forensics, and Strategies for University Management (Volume I and II) and Advances in Geoeconomics.* He directs consulting projects worldwide in the areas of strategy formulation, business development, and international finance.

Joobin Ordoobody has finished two years of PhD research and coursework in International Management and Organization at Gustavson School of Business, University of Victoria, where he was awarded the Faculty of Graduate Studies Fellowship in 2014. He also provides consulting for "Beewaz," a major art review online database in Iran. His main research areas include Organizational theory, international business, and creative industries.

Alireza Saify is a management scholar with an MSc in Public Administration. His research focuses on institutional theory, specifically the transaction between corporations and institutional logics.

Musicologist **Mark C. Samples** currently teaches music history and arts entrepreneurship at Central Washington University, and researches the role of branding and promotion in music after 1800, from Jenny Lind to Joan Baez, Tom Waits and Sufjan Stevens. Outside of the classroom, Dr Samples creates arts entrepreneurship tools and training for student and professional musicians, such as his workshop, "Branding for Musicians." At his current position, and previously as a Coleman Faculty Fellow in Entrepreneurship at Millikin University, he has led teams of student musicians in the process of designing entrepreneurial ventures that focus on value-creation.

Julienne (Julie) W. Shields obtained her BA in Classics from the University of Illinois, Urbana-Champaign, and her MBA from Millikin

University. Prior to joining Millikin, she spent 11 years in the information technology industry during which time she worked for Nims Associates, Inc. and owned two technology start-up businesses, Open Integration Incorporated which shared intellectual property with the University of Illinois and InVivo Ventures, LLC. In 2013 she joined Millikin University's faculty and in the commitment to Millikin's Performance Learning pedagogy led the Arts Entrepreneurship program including the Blue Connection retail art gallery learning laboratory for art and business students. Julie is currently the Director of the Center for Entrepreneurship and directs the Coleman Faculty Fellows program at Millikin University. She continues to foster the more than 15-year commitment to arts entrepreneurship and the development of artist entrepreneurs at the institution.

Aytug Sozuer is a lecturer of international business and entrepreneurship at University of Yalova, Turkey. He has a doctoral degree in Business Management and Organization from Istanbul University. Before joining academia, he worked at several multinational companies as a specialist in sales and exporting. His academic research fields of interest include governance, inter-firm relationships, and start-ups.

Larry Stapleton is an Associate professor of Operations Management at Millikin University in Decatur, IL, USA. He earned a BS in Applied Science from Miami University, an MBA from Chapman University, and a PhD in Decision Science with an emphasis in International Business from St. Louis University. He has served on the faculty at Millikin University since 2001. He has developed multiple international projects for students which are client based. He served in several engineering and management roles in Fortune 500 companies over 25 years before coming to Millikin. His current consulting and research is in the development of Quality Management Systems and the use of heuristic methodologies in developing solutions for logistic problems.

Todd A. Stuart is a Lecturer and the Director of the Arts Management & Entrepreneurship program at Miami University in Oxford, Ohio. He has over 20 years industry experience in the arts and entrepreneurship. In addition to his work at Miami, he is working on a start-up focused on helping practicing artists develop entrepreneurial skills. Todd holds an MBA and MFA from the University of South Carolina; and a BA from the University of Florida.

Sara Theis is an Assistant Professor of Stage Management and Theatre Administration at Millikin University. Since arriving at Millikin, she has been a Coleman Fellow and has spent a great deal of time focused in the area of Arts Entrepreneurship through her work with Pipe Dreams Studio Theatre. A member of Actors' Equity Association since 2001, Sara received her MFA from the University of Wisconsin-Milwaukee and her MBA from Millikin University.

Index

Announcing the Business Expert Press Digital Library

Concise e-books business students need for classroom and research

This book can also be purchased in an e-book collection by your library as

- a one-time purchase,
- that is owned forever,
- allows for simultaneous readers,
- has no restrictions on printing, and
- can be downloaded as PDFs from within the library community.

Our digital library collections are a great solution to beat the rising cost of textbooks. E-books can be loaded into their course management systems or onto students' e-book readers.
The **Business Expert Press** digital libraries are very affordable, with no obligation to buy in future years. For more information, please visit **www.businessexpertpress.com/librarians**. To set up a trial in the United States, please email **sales@businessexpertpress.com**.